The Fiery Dragon Gang

Ginger Ketting

Pacific Press Publishing Association
Boise, Idaho
Oshawa, Ontario, Canada

Edited by Bonnie Widicker
Designed by Tim Larson
Cover illustration by Bryant Eastman
Inside illustrations by Georgina Larson
Typeset in 11/13 Century Schoolbook

Copyright © 1991 by
Pacific Press Publishing Association
Printed in United States of America
All Rights Reserved

Library of Congress Catalog-in-Publication Data
Ketting, Ginger.
    p.   cm.
    Summary: When four children of missionaries in Malaysia form a club and treat an unpopular schoolmate as an enemy, the subsequent events bring one of them to a better understanding of how to treat people.
    ISBN 0-8163-1047-5
    1. Missionary stories. 2. Children of missionaries — Malaya—Juvenile literature. 3. Missions — Malaya—Juvenile literature. 4. Malaya — Church history — Juvenile literature. [1. Christian life.] I. Title.
BV2087.K47 1991   90-23386
266'.67595—dc20   CIP
                                                          AC

The Fiery Dragon Gang

Dedication

This book is lovingly dedicated to Leslie and Linda Dunston, my two students who kept begging for "another one of your stories from when you were a little girl, Miss Ketting."

It is also dedicated to my multigrade 3-5 class at Redlands Junior Academy, who kept insisting that I finish writing this book so they could hear it at storytime.

Melissa Casey, Erika DuBose, Kevin Lehmann, Rosie Neuharth, Allison Schmidt, Kimberly Sogioka, Becky Szumski, Jason Yapshing, Benji DuBose, Sierra Hausman, Loryn Hebert, Shawndra Hogle, Chris Santana, Todd Abercrombie, Bobby Chitrathorn, David Hadley, Robyn Hebert, Janelle Johns, Justin Kim, Paul Moorhead, Elisa Ramos, Michael Sogioka, Eddie Szumski, Aaron Testerman, and Tony Troncoso.

To each of these, I wish the talent of including everyone around them in their friendships, thus sharing even more fully Jesus' love.

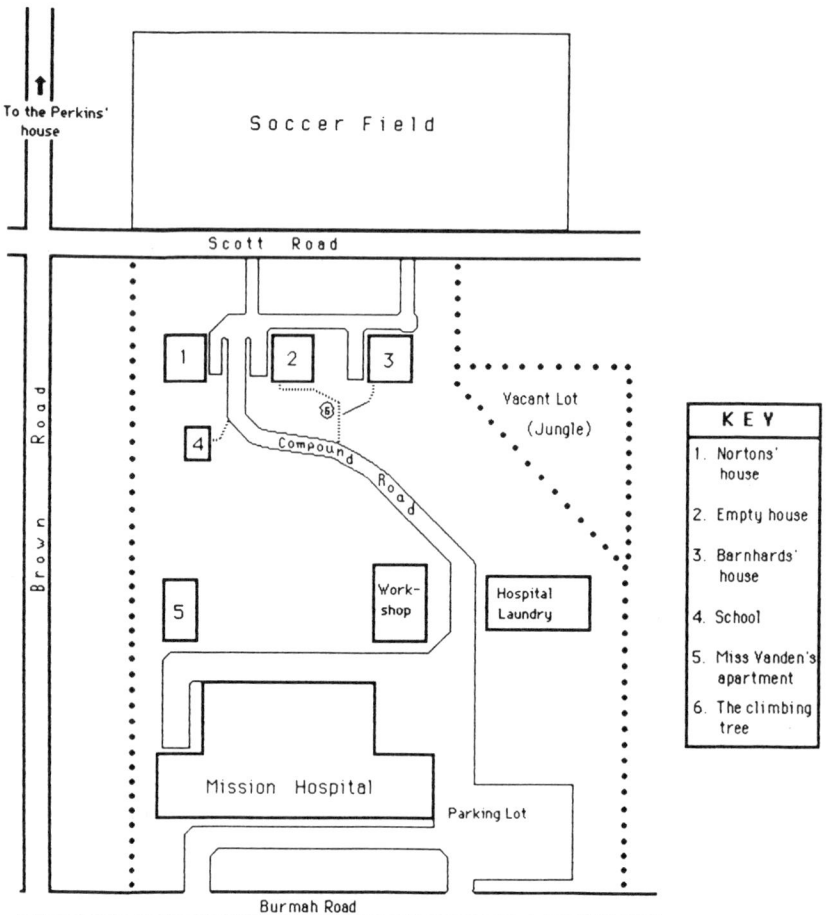

Contents

Chapter 1.	Mum's the Word	9
Chapter 2.	The Coconut Hut	17
Chapter 3.	The Jungle Clubhouse	25
Chapter 4.	The Biscuit-Tin Rocket	33
Chapter 5.	The Underground Hideout	43
Chapter 6.	Seven-Up's Ladder	53
Chapter 7.	April Fools' Pranks	62
Chapter 8.	The Japanese Fort Expedition	73
Chapter 9.	Deadwater Rafting	85
Chapter 10.	The Fight	95
Chapter 11.	Turned Tables	106
Chapter 12.	Do Unto Others	117

1
Mum's the Word

If Addie Barnhard had been a kitten, she would have purred. School was over for the day, and her piano practicing was done. The rest of the afternoon belonged to her, and she knew exactly what she was going to do with it. Turning the ceiling fan switch up a couple of notches to chase off the humid Malaysian heat, she curled up on the couch with a Marcia Green book and a bowl of fresh chilled rambutans. Rambutans are hairy red tropical fruit, about the size of a golf ball, which tastes a little like a cross between a peach and nectarine. The Barnhards' housemaid, Cecelia, had already peeled the rambutans that had grown on mission hospital trees. Seeing a few remaining ants on some of the rambutans, Addie made a mental note to avoid them—an ant could taste like a hot dash of chili pepper on your tongue. Addie popped a juicy rambutan into her mouth as she found her place in the book. The rambutan bulged out like a giant gumball in her cheek as its sweet, cool juice slowly trickled down her throat. Mmmmmm!

Addie soon forgot the rambutans as the story took her far from her home on the Malaysian island of Penang. The Marcia Green mystery books contained fascinating stories about a group of English children who organized themselves into a club called "The Daring Detectives." The five

THE FIERY DRAGON GANG

children in the stories were always stumbling across dark, shady characters with crooked scars or sinister looks. Going through exciting adventures and dangerous escapes, the Daring Detectives always helped the police catch the crooks. Often the criminals just happened to be on the police department's most-wanted list. Addie loved reading about how the children always figured things out, how daring and ingenious they were in solving the mysteries.

Addie's mother, a missionary doctor, wasn't too happy about Addie's reading Marcia Green books. One day she had paged through one of the books. It described the time the Daring Detectives had caught a bank robber when they were spending their school holidays at the seaside. They had noticed a suspicious-looking man lurking around the empty, boarded-up house next door and had spied on him. They took down the license plate number of the car he drove and staked out corners in the nearby seaside village to spy on his comings and goings.

"Addie," Dr. Barnhard had said, giving her daughter that I-don't-approve look, "this really isn't the kind of stuff I want you to be reading."

"Oh, Mama," Addie cajoled, "the Perkinses have a whole bunch of these books, and Nathan and Paul get to read them all the time."

"Well, this just doesn't look like uplifting reading material," Dr. Barnhard remarked. "I don't know why Mrs. Perkins lets her boys read these books."

"Mama, there isn't anything bad in them," Addie said as convincingly as she could. "The kids in this book catch a bank robber—they're good kids."

Dr. Barnhard sighed and handed the book back to Addie. "Well, I want you to learn to choose good reading material, Addie," she said. "I think we have better books here at home for you to read."

"But, Mama," Addie said, "I've read all the books here at home."

"I know, Addie," replied her mother with a smile. "That's one problem with living in the mission field—there is no Christian bookstore here in Penang where we can buy books. It's a good thing that we're going on vacation to America this summer. We can pick out some new books while we're there."

Addie's conversation with her mom flashed through her mind now as she flipped the page of her book, and a little feeling of guilt niggled at her. "But Mama didn't say I absolutely *can't* read these books," she thought, pushing her guilt aside. "After all, Nathan and Paul are missionary kids, too, and their mom doesn't mind if they read mystery books." Addie nibbled the last of the rambutan fruit off its seed, spit out the seed, and popped a fresh rambutan into her mouth. Tucking a strand of her wavy blond hair behind her ear, she sighed with satisfaction as she settled back into her story.

The *chirrr* of a rotating bicycle chain outside the front window brought Addie back into the real world. She hopped up and adjusted the dusty glass louvres of the windows so she could see out. There was Paul Perkins, just making a U-turn on his bicycle in front of the Barnhards' house. Looking down the road, Addie saw Nathan riding toward Paul.

"Hey, Nathan! Paul!" Addie called through the window screen. "What are you guys doing? Where are you going?" She stepped to the front door, slid the bolt aside, and ran down the front steps.

Nathan rode up, jamming on his brakes so that his back tire lifted off the road a couple of inches. His blond hair shone in the afternoon sunshine, and his face had

11

THE FIERY DRAGON GANG

turned a blotchy red from the heat and the exercise. He was wearing the shorts, shirt, and sandals with knee socks that the Australian kids usually wore. "We're just riding around," he informed Addie in his Australian accent. "Mum said we could come over and play awhile. Reckon you and Con can come out and ride bikes?"

"Yeah, we can," Addie said. She heard the thud of bare feet on the stairs behind her and looked up to see her younger brother, Con. He was wearing shorts, as usual, with a red-and-blue striped shirt.

"Addie, did you finish your practicing?" Con asked.

"Yes, I did," Addie replied, feeling a little irritated that Con was checking up on her. "Did you do yours?"

"Yep! At lunchtime," Con said.

"Come on, you two," Paul interrupted impatiently. "Get your bikes and come ride."

Addie and Con went to get their bikes. They were parked underneath the back steps of their mission house, which was built on stilts to raise it off the ground. Underneath the house stood boxes and boxes of disposable diapers stacked there by the hospital workshop men. Someone in America had shipped them over for the hospital nursery. The children pushed them around now and then, creating tunnels and rooms. Addie, glancing at them now, thought of their pretend games of adventure in those tunnels. That reminded her of the book she had just been reading.

"Hey, Nathan," Addie called. "I'm nearly finished with your Marcia Green book. I'll get it back to you tomorrow."

"Right," replied Nathan cheerfully. "Jolly good one, isn't it?"

"Sure is," Addie agreed. Her bicycle tires bumped across the narrow open drain around the Barnhards'

MUM'S THE WORD

house as she walked her bike out to the driveway.

"Nathan, may I read it after Addie?" Con asked. "I haven't read that one yet."

"Sure," Nathan said.

"Hey, you guys!" Addie exclaimed, stopping still in her tracks. "Wouldn't it be fun if we could have a club like the Daring Detectives? Just think of all the things we could do!"

"Yeah!" Paul stopped walking his bike, his face brightening. He peered through his thick glasses at the other children, his brown hair tousled above his eyebrows. "We could catch crooks and get the rewards and stuff like that."

"Don't be a twit, Paul." Nathan glanced at his younger brother with disdain. "That's just stuff you read in the books." He paused thoughtfully, and then a gleam of interest flashed in his eyes as he added, "We could make a club, though. We could have a clubhouse and do stuff, like the Daring Detectives."

"And we could have officers of our club, like the Daring Detectives did," said Con, picking up on the idea.

"And we could have a secret password," added Nathan. His mind was obviously churning quickly now.

"Yeah," said Addie, pleased that her idea had caught on with Nathan. He was the oldest of the children and usually invented the fun ideas when they were playing. "We could figure out a good name for ourselves and find mysteries to solve, like the Daring Detectives."

"But there's only four of us," said Paul.

"Well, we won't call ourselves the Daring Detectives," said Nathan. "We'll think of a new name. And anyway, Joel can be in our club too." Joel was Nathan and Paul's little brother, who was too young to be in school.

"What about Jerry and Kamie Norton?" asked Con,

THE FIERY DRAGON GANG

referring to the other missionary kids in their church school.

"I don't like Jerry," said Paul. "He stuck out his tongue at me during recess today. I don't think we should allow a cheeky boy like him to be in our club."

"Anyway," Nathan continued as though it were already decided, "a club must have an enemy or somebody to spy on. I think Jerry should be our enemy. And Kamie couldn't be in our club because she would go and tell her brother everything we do. She's only five years old anyhow, so she's not much use."

Addie didn't think that *enemy* sounded like a word Christian children should use to describe their classmate, even if he was "cheeky," as Paul put it. But then she remembered that the day before, she and Mama had looked out their window and had seen Jerry get mad at Kamie over something. Angry voices had risen from the driveway. Then Jerry took hold of his little sister by the neck and shook her viciously. Mama had run downstairs and ordered him to stop hurting his little sister. She made him go home while Kamie stayed to play with Addie for a while. Remembering Jerry's meanness to his little sister, Addie kept her mouth shut about Nathan's choice of Jerry for the club "enemy."

Nathan's voice broke into Addie's thoughts. "How about a club meeting right now to organize ourselves?"

"OK," said Addie, eager not to be left out. "We need a notebook and pencil to write things down. Let's meet in our backyard." The children all turned and raced back to the Barnhards' yard, stopping long enough to lean their bikes against the house stilts. Addie dashed up to her room to get a notebook and pencil. Then she joined the others on the grass. Tammy, Addie's dachshund dog, scurried up and tried to lick Addie's chin. Addie stroked

Tammy's brown, wiry fur and turned her head to avoid her puppy's happy, wet licks.

"Addie, write down the name of our club. It's the Fiery Dragon Gang," said Con.

"Hey, you guys went ahead without me!" Addie complained.

"It's a jolly good name, I think," Nathan announced as Paul nodded in agreement.

"It sounds fierce," commented Addie as she wrote "FIERY DRAGON GANG" at the top of the page. Then she looked up. "Now we need officers."

"I nominate Nathan for leader," said Con.

"Me too," Paul said, pushing his glasses up on his nose.

"Right, then. I'll be the leader," said Nathan. Addie wrote down "Leader: Nathan P."

"Well, since I'm already doing it, I could be the secretary," said Addie.

"Fine," said Nathan. Addie wrote "Secretary: Addie B."

"I want to draw a picture of a hot rod for the front page of our club book," said Con.

"What for?" Addie asked. "Our gang doesn't have anything to do with a hot rod."

"It will be the Fiery Dragon Gang hot rod." Con shifted his legs out of their crossed position.

"But we *don't* have a hot rod," Addie protested.

"Let him draw it, Addie," Nathan advised. "It will make a nice front page for our book. Now write on the next line: 'Enemy: Jerry Norton.' "

"I don't think we should call him our enemy," Addie protested. "I don't want Jerry in our club either, but that's not a very nice name."

"Well, he's mean," said Nathan. "And what's the good

15

THE FIERY DRAGON GANG

of a club if we don't have people who aren't in our club?"

Addie thought a moment. "Then I'll write 'People not in our club,' " she persisted.

"OK," Nathan said. "Suit yourself. So, then, we all agree. I'm the leader of the Fiery Dragon Gang, and Addie, you're the secretary. And Con, Paul, and Joel are in the club, but Jerry and Kamie aren't."

"Got it," said Addie, scribbling down the last name.

"Let's go ride bikes now." Paul got up, tired of sitting on the grass. "We can do more Fiery Dragon Gang stuff later."

"Right," replied Nathan, jumping up. "But remember, Mum's the word. This is a deep dark secret from everyone, especially Jerry."

Addie nodded solemnly along with the others. She handed the notebook to Con. "Put this in the house, Con. You can draw your picture later."

Con dashed up the back stairs two at a time as the other children put up the kickstands on their bikes. "I'll be right out," he called. "Wait for me." The children were soon pedaling off with thoughts of their newly formed club buzzing around in their heads.

2
The Coconut Hut

With school, piano lessons, and swimming lessons to pay attention to, the children didn't think much about the Fiery Dragon Gang for a while. Con drew a fine-looking hot rod in the Fiery Dragon Gang notebook, and then Addie left the book on the dresser in her room. It lay there for several days. Addie would see the notebook on her dresser in the mornings and then forget to remind the boys of it at school. But then one morning something happened to get them back on track. Addie was the first to notice it as she ate her breakfast at the back porch dining table.

Up the narrow road through the hospital compound came a little procession of Indian men. Several of them pushed carts while others walked behind them. Each man wore a mean-looking knife hanging from a special belt and carried a circle of rope over his shoulder. Each had tied a bandanna around his head. And each man was barefoot.

"Hey, Con!" Addie called to her brother. "Come look! The men are coming to harvest coconuts today!"

Con appeared around the corner and entered the kitchen. He pulled the cereal box out of the cupboard and the milk out of the fridge. Addie and Con's mother had already been called to the mission hospital to deliver a baby.

THE COCONUT HUT

Their dad had gone to do surgery while they were still asleep. The children were on their own for breakfast, but they were used to managing that. Con settled himself at the dining room table. After a quick blessing, he gazed out the window at the coconut harvesters. "I hope Miss Vanden lets us watch them at recess time," he commented, following his words with a heaping bite of cereal.

The voices of the men drifted through the morning air as they organized their things under the bungah rayah tree. Two men broke away from the group and strolled up the Barnhards' walkway and through the gap in the hedge. They stopped by the backyard pond and peered into the murky green water. The pond contained golden carp, but the Indian men would never know it, because the fish rarely surfaced. As the children watched, the men turned their attention to the tall coconut tree beside the pond.

"Oh, good," Addie remarked. "They're going to do our tree first." She paused for another bite of cereal. "I wonder what would happen if the men never harvested the coconuts."

"Probably the coconuts would fall by themselves and hit someone on the head," Con said.

"Ouch!" Addie reacted. "I suppose so. And our tree isn't very safe, because the back walkway goes right by it." She leaned back to open the screen door behind her for Tammy, who had been pawing at it for the last few minutes. Happy at being let into the house, the dog dashed in and started snuffling around the children's legs, her toenails clicking on the tile floor.

Outside, one of the men walked up to the tree trunk and bent over as he slipped a loop of thick rope around his ankles. Straightening up, he circled the tree with his arms and then drew his legs up under him. He braced

19

THE FIERY DRAGON GANG

the soles of his feet against each side of the trunk. The rope held his feet firmly spaced apart. Standing with his feet on each side of the trunk, he shifted his arm grasp higher up on the trunk. Then up came his feet again, and like an inchworm he climbed up the tree: arms up, feet up, arms up, feet up.

"Boy, I wish I could do that," Con said admiringly.

"Me too," Addie agreed.

When he reached the coconuts thirty feet up on the tree, the man freed one hand to grasp the knife in his belt. Pulling it out, he chopped at the stem above one coconut until it suddenly cut loose and plummeted to the ground. The other man stood well away from the base of the tree, watching his partner. *Hack, hack, hack,* went the knife. *Plop, plop, plop.* The coconuts fell one by one, rolling across the lawn as they hit. Then the climber stopped and rested for a while as he hollered down to his friend on the ground.

"He's going to cut off the lower palm fronds next," Addie said, "and then he'll be done."

"I know, and then we can use them to make a coconut hut," Con added.

"Hey, yeah! Let's build one at lunch hour!" Addie exclaimed. It was one of the things the children always looked forward to at coconut harvesting time.

Just then the children heard a bell clanging. "Five minutes till school starts!" exclaimed Con, picking up his dish and plopping it into the kitchen sink. "We'd better hurry!" Addie scurried after him, with Tammy at her heels. The children ran down the back path, pausing first to make sure no coconuts or fronds were falling. They hurried along the back hedge to the school.

"Hey, you guys! Hurry up!" Paul Perkins called from the school door where he stood, bell in hand. "I'm going

THE COCONUT HUT

to ring the last bell in twenty seconds." Addie and Con rushed in and plunked down in their chairs, panting, as Paul began swinging the bell back and forth wildly outside the school door.

Nathan tilted back in his chair from the desk in front of Addie. "Have you been watching the men harvest coconuts?" he asked.

"Yeah. They just started a little while ago. You guys want to make a coconut hut at lunch time?"

"Mum said we're supposed to eat at the hospital cafeteria today, so we'll have time." The Perkinses lived off the hospital compound, so it usually took the Perkins boys the full lunch hour to ride home on their bikes, eat lunch, and ride back to school.

"Good! Oops, we'd better be quiet," warned Addie as she looked up and saw Miss Vanden giving her the look that meant "settle down for worship."

During school time the children could hear the sounds of the coconut harvest going on outside the windows. Paul stopped by one window to watch the men. After a few minutes Miss Vanden noticed and told him to go to his seat and get busy. Reluctantly, he wandered back to his desk and flopped into his chair.

At recess the children watched as two of the men tied their knives to the top of short poles they had pounded into the ground. With the knife blades pointing up, they took the coconuts one by one and jammed them down on the knives, expertly peeling off the outer husks like sections of an orange. They threw the nuts into a cart that was attached to a bicycle and threw the husks into a pile nearby. The pile of husks grew quickly.

Jerry Norton, the newest missionary kid in school, hadn't seen coconut harvest before. His freckled nose twitched with interest as he watched. "How come they

THE FIERY DRAGON GANG

take the outside off?" he asked, tilting his head with the question.

"Because they want only the nuts to sell," said Con.

"And then we get to play with the husks," said Addie. "If you stack them up like igloo blocks, you can make a great hut."

"Oh," said Jerry slowly. It didn't sound as if he understood.

"You'll see," said Nathan with a superior sniff. "We're going to make a coconut hut, and you can watch if you like."

Cecelia, the Barnhards' housemaid, had fried rice waiting for the children when they got home at noon. Addie and Con bolted their lunch and ran outside to where the mound of coconut husks lay by the gardeners' garage.

"Here, Con. Let's pick up as many of these as we can carry and build our hut over there." Addie pointed to a level spot on the lawn. The children began hauling coconut husks, building a new pile by their chosen spot. Then Addie let Con do the carrying while she laid the husks end to end in a square for the base of the walls. She left a blank space where the door would go.

Soon Nathan came racing through the rambutan orchard from the hospital cafeteria, with Paul right behind him. The children started stacking the husks up like house bricks, each one overlapping two husks below it. Soon they had built the walls of their hut high enough that they could crawl around in the hut once they got the roof on. Con and Paul dragged coconut fronds over for the roof. While they were working, Jerry Norton and his little sister Kamie came running from their house and stood by, watching with great interest as the coconut hut grew. Jerry's red hair shone in the sunshine, and his freckles seemed to get darker the longer he stood there in the sun.

THE COCONUT HUT

Finally the children were ready to put the roof on the coconut hut. Carefully they lifted the palm fronds and placed them across the top of the husk walls, with the ends of the fronds hanging over on either side of the hut. It made a nice flat roof on the hut. After the fronds were in place, Addie crawled through the door of the hut and poked the leaves up from underneath so they wouldn't hang down into the hut. The hut felt nice and cozy, with the sweet smell of fresh coconut heavy in the air. Nathan and Paul crawled in behind Addie, and then Con and Jerry started through the door on hands and knees.

"Hey, you guys," Nathan yelled. "There isn't enough room in here for all of us. Wait until we get out, and then you can have your turn."

Con and Jerry backed away from the doorway, and Paul crawled backward out of the hut to leave more room.

"Addie!" Nathan whispered, beckoning her close with his finger. Addie crawled over to him, wondering what he wanted. "Remember our club?" Nathan asked. "We can make a coconut hut clubhouse this afternoon. We'll do it secretly so Jerry and Kamie won't know."

Addie's eyes widened. "That's a good idea. But we have to make it in a good place where Jerry can't find it."

"I'll call my mum after school and get permission to stay over here and play," Nathan said. "We can figure it out then."

"Hey, it's our turn now. Get out of there so we can come in," Jerry shouted from outside. Nathan and Addie crawled out of the hut. Nathan gave Addie a knowing smirk as they stood up. Jerry noticed it. "All right, what's the secret?" he demanded.

"Oh, nothing," Nathan said mysteriously. Con had already disappeared through the door of the coconut hut.

THE FIERY DRAGON GANG

Jerry followed him, seeing that he wasn't going to get a good answer from Nathan. Paul dived in through the door behind them while Kamie hung back. "Start thinking of how to do it," Nathan whispered to Addie.

Addie saw Kamie's puzzled look as she watched them, so she kept silent. But her mind began to work on places for the Fiery Dragon Gang clubhouse.

Just then the first bell rang for the afternoon session of school. Jerry, Paul, and Con scrambled out of the hut, and all the children started walking toward school except for Kamie, who ran off toward home. Her straight, long blond hair swung back and forth across her back as she ran.

As they walked in the school door, Nathan looked at Addie and grinned. Addie raised her eyebrows at him to let him know she knew what he was thinking about. The Fiery Dragon Gang would be busy that afternoon!

3
The Jungle Clubhouse

After school Nathan arrived at the Barnhard house to phone his mother for permission to stay and play. "Yeah, Mum. We'll be home by dinnertime," Addie heard him tell his mother.

"All right!" Con exclaimed as Nathan hung up the receiver. "Where will we make our clubhouse?"

"This could be difficult," Nathan said. "We need a place where Jerry won't be able to find us."

"Well, there are those boxes of the hospital's diapers that are stored underneath our house," Con offered. "We've played in there before."

"That's exactly why we *shouldn't* make our clubhouse in there," Nathan declared. "Jerry has played with us among the boxes before. He'd come snooping around there, first thing."

"Well, I wanted to use the coconut husks to make our clubhouse," grumbled Addie. "That means we have to build it out on the compound and not somewhere like under our house. Why don't we just walk around the compound and look for a place?" Without waiting for someone to agree, she headed out the door. The boys followed behind.

The children started at the Barnhards' house and walked down the compound road past the empty house

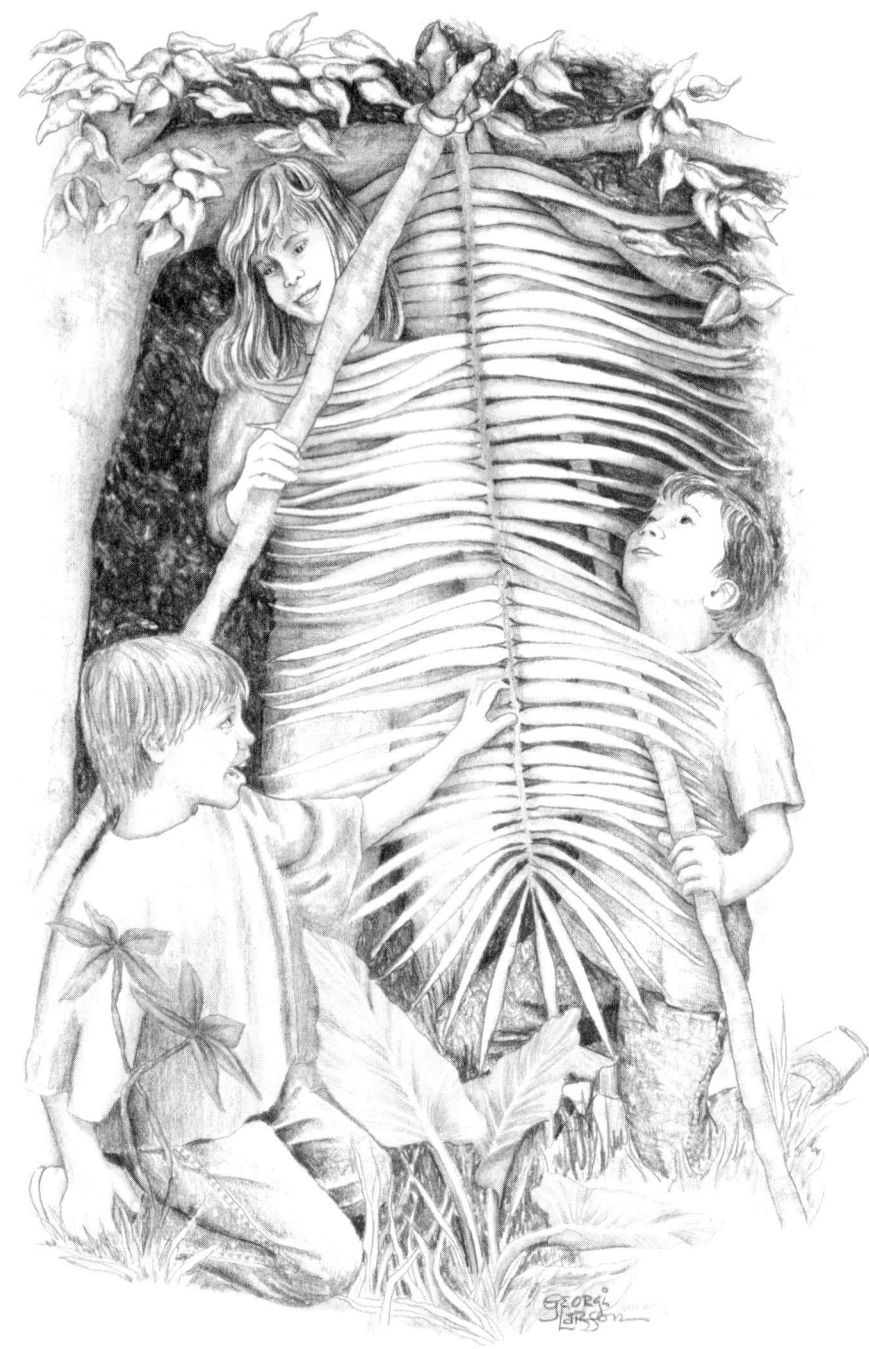

THE JUNGLE CLUBHOUSE

next door and the Nortons' house. The neatly mowed lawns made the compound look so open; there didn't seem to be any place to hide a clubhouse. Rounding the corner, the children wandered past the school, the rambutan orchard, and the gardeners' garage. As they approached the hospital laundry, Nathan stopped. His eyes narrowed as he inspected the compound fence by the laundry. Beyond the fence lay a small lot overgrown with trees, bushes, weeds, and vines. It came very close to being a tropical jungle.

"I wish we could put our clubhouse in that jungle," Nathan commented. "Jerry would never think to look for us there."

"That's off the compound," warned Addie. "It's not even our land."

"But nobody goes there," said Con. "Nathan, there's a hole under our back fence, you know. We can crawl under the fence and get into the jungle."

"Well, what are we waiting for!" Nathan exclaimed, and he took off running. Addie, Con, and Paul raced after him. They burst through a gap in the Barnhards' backyard hedge, stopped, and looked around.

"Right over here," Con directed, panting. He walked past their avocado tree growing out of a huge anthill, and led them to the back corner of the yard, to where the hedge met the barbed-wire fence. There, at the bottom of the fence, was a small hole, which the neighborhood dogs used as they wandered around. Con got down on his stomach and scooched under the bottom strand of barbed wire.

"Careful, Con," Addie warned, worrying about their intrusion into the jungle lot. Nathan followed Con, with Paul right behind him. Addie gingerly lowered herself down on her stomach and started under the barbed wire.

27

THE FIERY DRAGON GANG

She paused. "Somebody hold the wire up above me," she pleaded. Paul took the wire between his thumb and index finger and lifted it up as far as he could. Addie wriggled under and stood up on the other side, brushing dirt off her dress.

"Come on," Nathan urged, heading off through the undergrowth. The other children followed him in single file, watching carefully where they placed each step. They knew they should watch out for snakes in a place like this.

Suddenly Addie jumped as Nathan let out a yell. "Hey! Here's the perfect place!"

The children rushed forward to see what he had found. Nathan stood on a bare patch of ground under a rambutan tree that hung over the fence between the jungle and the hospital compound. The fence was covered with vines. A branch of the rambutan tree above the children paralleled the ground. Tall undergrowth surrounded the bare patch of ground under the tree.

"Look at this!" Nathan exclaimed. "We could make walls with the coconut tree branches. If we lean them against that branch, it will be like a tepee inside."

"You know what else?" added Paul. "This place has great natural camouflage, with all these vines and stuff around. Jerry could never see us. And we can leave a secret emergency exit back there in case he ever comes nearby." He pointed to the trunk of the rambutan tree.

"This is a great place to spy through the fence on the hospital compound," Addie observed, looking through the weeds toward the laundry on the other side of the fence. "We can see people walk by, and no one will guess we're watching them."

"Well." Nathan stood with his hands on his hips. "I say this is a jolly good place for our clubhouse. Let's go

THE JUNGLE CLUBHOUSE

get the coconut branches. We can chuck them over the fence and come back afterward and set them up."

The children raced for the fence and scooted back under. Con's shirt caught on the barbed wire and would have torn, but Addie caught him in time and unhooked it from the barb.

Back at the stack of coconut branches, the children each grabbed two branches and started dragging them over to the fence. It took some effort to heave them up over the high fence. Addie handed the branches to the boys, who worked together to chuck the branches over.

The children had been working for a few minutes when Jerry and Kamie strolled around the bend in the road from their house. Seeing the other children hard at work, they ran up to investigate.

"What are you doing?" Jerry asked.

Addie looked at Nathan. Jerry was their club enemy. They couldn't tell him they were building a clubhouse. What would they say?

"What are you doing?" Jerry repeated, stretching up on tiptoe as he tried to see over the fence.

"Throwing branches over the fence, can't you see?" replied Nathan rudely.

"What for?" Jerry asked.

"To help the gardeners clean up the compound," Nathan answered glibly.

"That's a lie," Addie thought. Suddenly she felt very uncomfortable. She knew she was taking part in the lie just by being there and not saying anything.

"You're helping the gardeners clean up?" Jerry asked, watching Con throw a coconut frond over the fence.

"Well, we're just doing it because we want to," Addie blurted, before Nathan could say anything else. She glanced at Nathan. He didn't seem to notice. "At least

THE FIERY DRAGON GANG

that wasn't quite a lie," she thought.

"Can we help too?" Jerry asked.

Nathan thought a second. "Sure, if you want to." A smirk began to spread across his face.

Jerry didn't see the smirk, but Con, Paul, and Addie did. Addie giggled as Jerry and Kamie ran off to get some coconut fronds. When they were out of hearing, Paul laughed out loud. "That's pretty good, Nathan," he told his brother, "getting them to help us build our clubhouse. And they don't even know they're doing it!"

For a while Jerry and Kamie helped the other children. Then Nathan announced, "That's enough for now. Let's quit."

"What will we do now?" Jerry threw the last frond over the fence and looked at Nathan.

"It's time for you to go home," Nathan told him. "We don't want to play with you anymore."

Addie stared at Nathan, shocked at his boldness.

"We don't have to go home if we don't want to," Jerry protested.

Kamie looked puzzled and unhappy. She was too little to understand what was happening, but she knew that Nathan wanted them to go away. Kamie turned to her brother. "Jerry, let's go home," she said. She tugged on his elbow.

Jerry started toward home with his sister. Addie caught the hurt looks on their faces as they turned to go. She felt a little guilty, watching them walk home. Of course they couldn't put up their clubhouse with Jerry around. But she knew it had been downright mean to tell Jerry to go away.

When Jerry and Kamie were out of sight, the children headed for the hole under the fence. They scrambled through the jungle and began propping up the coconut fronds against the rambutan tree branch. The children left a space back by the tree trunk for an emergency escape hatch. They stomped the weeds down on the ground to make the floor and checked to make sure several peepholes were available through the vines covering the fence. Paul climbed the tree and established a lookout in the branches.

The children's plans proceeded nicely, but as they worked, Addie felt an uncomfortable feeling in her stomach over how they had treated Jerry and Kamie. And somehow it spoiled the fun of building their Fiery Dragon Gang clubhouse.

4
The Biscuit-Tin Rocket

The Fiery Dragon Gang used their jungle clubhouse a few times after they built it, but it wasn't very useful once it was all set up. For one thing, the children couldn't think of anything to do there. They could just sit around or climb the rambutan tree. And the clubhouse wasn't much good for spying on Jerry Norton. He and Kamie usually played at their own house, out of sight from the jungle clubhouse. The only thing the Fiery Dragon Gang children could see, peering between the weeds and through the fence, was the laundry, the gardeners' garage, and the school. Hardly anyone interesting walked or drove by. It was just plain boring.

But then one day something happened at school that got the Fiery Dragon Gang cranked up and ready to go again. It all began in science class.

"How many of you think you'd like to travel in space someday?" Miss Vanden asked at the beginning of class. Nearly every hand went up.

"I'm not going to space," Paul announced. "I'm going to be a mad scientist and invent a purple cow when I grow up." Paul always said that whenever someone asked what he would be when he grew up.

Miss Vanden didn't reply to Paul's comment. "What would you need to travel in space?" she asked.

THE FIERY DRAGON GANG

"A rocket," answered Con. "And a spacesuit."

"And some oxygen," added Paul.

"Good answers," said Miss Vanden. "Do any of you know who made the first rockets?"

No hands went up. "It was the Chinese," said Miss Vanden. "They invented firecrackers and rockets many years ago."

"Yeah," Paul broke in. "Like the firecrackers at Chinese New Year. Bang! Bang! Bam-bam-bam!"

"We don't need the sound effects, Paul," said Miss Vanden with a stern look. She continued with the lesson. "Today we are going to learn about the father of modern rocketry and space flight. His name was Robert Goddard. Robert Goddard began inventing modern rockets when he was still a student. He developed propellant pumps. They pump fuel to the combustion chambers of rockets. He also developed gyrocontrols and instruments for guiding rockets." Miss Vanden paused. The children listened attentively, especially the boys, who liked things like rockets. "Look in your science books at the diagram showing what makes up a rocket," Miss Vanden directed the children. "What parts go together to make up a rocket? . . . Jerry, your hand was up."

"Well, there has to be a fuel tank, liquid oxygen, and a combustion chamber," said Jerry, reading from the diagram.

"What else, Paul?" Miss Vanden asked Paul, whose hand waved back and forth in the air.

"A cone at the top and nozzles," Paul answered, his eyes glinting behind his thick glasses, "so the exhaust can come out the back. Pshshshshshsh!" He made the sound to go with an imaginary rocket. Putting his hands together as if they were a rocket, he pretended to launch them from his desk into the air.

THE BISCUIT-TIN ROCKET

"Paul!" Miss Vanden's voice carried a stern warning tone.

"Oops!" said Paul, clamping his hand over his mouth. The other children could see the twinkle in his eyes, even through his thick glasses.

Nathan's hand was up. "Miss Vanden?" He waited for her to nod at him. "You said Robert Goddard made a rocket when he was a student?"

"Yes!" Miss Vanden looked pleased that Nathan had listened so carefully. "He tried over and over and kept making improvements on it."

Nathan nodded and didn't say anything more. The science lesson continued.

After school the subject of rockets came up again. Nathan, Paul, Addie, and Con were leaving school when Nathan stopped Con with a hand on his shoulder. "Let's make a rocket. We can make it the Fiery Dragon Gang rocket."

Addie looked from one of the boys to the other. A rocket? Who ever heard of making a rocket? Only engineers at Cape Canaveral in Florida could build rockets. How did Nathan think that the Fiery Dragon Gang was going to build a rocket all by themselves?

Con didn't seem to think Nathan's idea was such an impossible one. "OK," he said, looking rather interested. "How do we make it?"

"Well, let's see. Does your dad have stuff in his workshop to make it?"

"Sure! At least I guess so. Let's go find out what he has." Con started off for home, with Paul and Nathan behind.

"Hey, where are you going?" called Jerry, coming out the school door.

"Somewhere. And you're not invited," yelled Nathan

THE FIERY DRAGON GANG

over his shoulder.

Addie saw a flash of hurt cross Jerry's face. Then, noticing that she was watching him, Jerry stuck his tongue out in the direction of the other boys. Shrugging, he turned toward home.

Addie walked more slowly toward her own house. She wasn't terribly excited about rocketry, but she didn't want to be left out, either. When she arrived at home, the boys were already in Dr. Barnhard's workshop, scrounging around for materials to use in rocket building.

"We need something to use for the main part of the rocket," Con said, poking here and there in his father's scraps. He didn't seem to find anything on the shelves or tables, except some pop-bottle caps. "We can use these for nozzles on the bottom of the rocket," he suggested. "But we still need something for the main body."

Addie squinched up her eyes and thought hard for a minute. "I know!" she exclaimed suddenly. "Mama has a tall tin can of digestive biscuits upstairs in the kitchen cupboard. We could take the biscuits out and use the tin!" She ran up the back stairs, through the dining room, and into the kitchen, where she got the tin can out of the cupboard. Taking the lid off the top, Addie shook the English biscuits out onto the kitchen counter. Then she ran back down to the workshop with the tin and its lid.

"That's just the thing." Nathan grabbed the tin from Addie, and they set to work. On a shelf the boys found a glass jar to use for the fuel tank. It fit snugly into the tin, but it took up most of the space. They nailed the pop-bottle caps on the bottom of the tin to look like nozzles and found a piece of cardboard to make into a cone for the top of the rocket.

"We can cut this in a triangle and fold it like this to make the cone," suggested Con.

36

THE BISCUIT-TIN ROCKET

"How will you attach the cone to the top of the tin?" Addie asked.

"Ta-ta!" Nathan sang out, waving a roll of tape in front of her. "Sticky tape!"

"Are you sure the cone won't come off?" Addie questioned.

"We'll use *lots* of sticky tape," Nathan replied confidently.

"What about liquid oxygen to combust with the fuel?" asked Paul suddenly.

"We don't have liquid oxygen, you twit," his brother replied.

"Twit yourself," Paul replied, giving his brother a little shove. "So what are you going to use?"

Nathan stood still and thought for a minute. This posed a problem. The science book clearly showed a tank of liquid oxygen in the rocket design. But the biscuit tin was already full with the glass jar for the fuel tank. The children looked at each other, wondering how to deal with their problem. "Well," said Nathan finally, "since we don't have liquid oxygen, the fuel will just have to combust with the air around it. After all, air is oxygen. It's just that air is in the form of gas, and who says it has to be in liquid form for the rocket to work properly?"

"What are you going to use for fuel?" inquired Addie.

"Gasoline is fuel. Do you have any gasoline?" Nathan asked.

Con looked around the workshop. "I don't know," he said, moving jars around on the shelves in order to look. "Sometimes my dad has some in here." He poked around among all the tools and tin cans and boxes of nails. "I can't find any," he said at last.

"Hey, we could ask Supayah!" Addie suggested. "He keeps gasoline in the gardeners' garage for the hospital

THE FIERY DRAGON GANG

lawn mowers." Addie knew that the gardeners would probably allow the missionary children to take whatever they wanted, as long as they didn't take too much of it.

The children dashed out of the workshop to look for Supayah, the Indian gardener. They found him sweeping up leaves under the bungah rayah tree. He wore his regular khaki uniform and thongs on his feet. His smile shone white in his dark face as he watched the children approach.

"Hey, Supayah," Nathan called. "Can we get gasoline from you? We need just a little." He held out the jar that was to fit in the rocket.

"Gasoline?" Supayah asked. His English was very poor.

"Yeah. You know, gas," said Nathan.

Supayah walked over and unlocked the padlock on the gardeners' garage, swinging back the big wooden door. Shuffling into the dark recesses of the garage, he rummaged around until he found what he was looking for: a tank of gasoline. He carefully poured a little bit into the jar for the children.

"Thank you," the children chorused, and they walked back to the Barnhards' workshop. Nathan took short little steps so as not to spill the gasoline. Carefully they placed the jar back into their rocket.

"Now we need a wick," Nathan said, "so we can light the gasoline. Do you guys have any string?"

"Here's some," replied Con, reaching behind a container of screws and pulling out a ball of twine. "Will this do?"

"I think so," said Nathan, using a pair of rusty scissors to cut off a long piece. "We must have a long wick, because we have to be quite far away before the fuel ignites. You know how they have to stay far away when

THE BISCUIT-TIN ROCKET

real rockets take off at Cape Canaveral."

"How far up do you think our rocket will go?" asked Paul.

"It better go pretty far, for all the work we've done on it," replied Nathan.

"Do you think it will reach outer space?" Paul asked.

"I hope it goes to the moon," said Addie. "Wouldn't it be neat if our rocket got as far as the moon? Maybe someday astronauts would discover it up there and wonder who sent it."

"The moon is pretty far away," Con said.

"Well, I think we're ready." Nathan sounded satisfied. "Now we need some sort of launching pad or something to keep the rocket straight up."

"We can set it up on these bricks," Con suggested, picking up two red bricks from beside the workshop door. Addie grabbed two more.

"Let's launch it in the big field across Scott Road," Nathan said, heading for the door as he carefully carried the rocket. "Oh." He stopped. "Matches. We need matches to light the wick."

"There." Con pointed with his chin. "They're up on that shelf." Paul got the matches, since he was the only one left with nothing to carry.

The children formed a little procession leaving the workshop. First went Nathan, carrying the rocket. Then came Addie and Con with two bricks each, and Paul followed, carrying the matches. They paraded from the Barnhards' house out to the back gate of the hospital compound. It was the gate the Perkins boys used when they rode their bikes to school every day.

"Paul, get the gate key out of my pocket," Nathan instructed, holding his elbow out so that Paul could reach his pocket. Paul fished the key out of Nathan's

THE FIERY DRAGON GANG

pocket and unlocked the gate. The children crossed the dirt road to the huge grassy field bordered by a ditch.

Nathan jumped across the dry ditch and walked out onto the field. "Here," he said. "Set up the bricks here." Addie and Con put down the bricks in stacks of two, and Nathan set the rocket up on them so that there was a space under it. He carefully laid the wick so that the free end came out and away from the rocket.

"Now get down in the ditch and wait while I light the wick," Nathan commanded. Con, Addie, and Paul squatted down in the ditch, watching Nathan strike the match. After several tries, one lighted up. Then it blew out.

Nathan licked his finger and held it up to see which direction the breeze was coming from. He turned his back to the wind so that the match would be protected this time. Again he struck a match. This one stayed lighted. Nathan bent and touched the flaming match to the wick. As soon as he saw it was burning, he ran for the ditch and jumped in beside the others. The children waited and watched. Nothing happened.

"I'd better go and look," Nathan said. "The fire on the wick may have gone out."

"Wait, Nathan," said Addie. "It might be just getting to the rocket, and it might take off when you're by it." The children waited a little longer. Still nothing happened. Nathan hopped out of the ditch and went to investigate.

"It's burned out," he called back. He lighted the wick again, this time closer to the rocket. Once he saw that it was burning, he ran for the ditch and squatted by the others.

Poof! The rocket leaped three feet up into the air, long orange flames blazing out from both the bottom and the

THE BISCUIT-TIN ROCKET

top. It hit the ground burning fiercely. Flames licked at the green grass around it, scorching it black. The children watched, their mouths hanging open.

"Wow!" Paul said in awe, watching from the ditch.

"It didn't go very high." Addie was disappointed.

"Boy, it's really burning!" Con exclaimed.

"Not bad," Nathan commented.

"What in the world do you children think you're doing?" An angry voice came from the hospital compound. The children whirled around to see Mr. Watson, the hospital business manager, striding toward the gate.

"Uh oh," Nathan muttered under his breath.

"I think we're in trouble," whispered Paul.

It was Addie who spoke up at last. "We made a rocket," she explained as Mr. Watson crossed the road and walked up to the ditch.

"And why is it burning like that?" Mr. Watson asked sternly, standing with his hands on his hips.

"We used gasoline," said Paul. "It didn't go up very far. It's just burning up."

"Where did you get gasoline?" asked Mr. Watson.

"From Supayah's garage," said Nathan.

Mr. Watson sighed in exasperation. "You children could have been killed or badly burned," he said. "Did you know that? That was a stupid thing to do, lighting gasoline. You're lucky it didn't explode that can into a thousand bits. Your parents would have been cutting pieces of shrapnel out of all of you in the hospital." He looked grimly over at the blackened biscuit tin. The fire was pretty much burned out by now, although the grass was still smoking.

The children didn't say a word. Addie felt that lumpy I-am-in-BIG-trouble feeling in the pit of her stomach. She was beginning to realize the meaning of Mr.

41

THE FIERY DRAGON GANG

Watson's words. It really had been a foolish thing to do.

"Well, you'd better get back into the compound," said Mr. Watson. Nathan headed over toward the burned rocket. "No, Nathan!" Mr. Watson warned. "Don't pick it up. It will still be so hot, you'll burn your hands. Come on, back onto the compound." He walked over and stomped on the scorched grass to be sure the fire was out.

The children silently filed through the gate. Mr. Watson stopped to lock it behind them. "I'll be talking to Supayah about this," he said. His final words were, "Don't you *ever* play with gasoline again!"

"We won't," the children promised.

5
The Underground Hideout

The sun beat down fiercely from a cloudless sky one Sunday morning. Not a breath of wind stirred to give relief from the muggy island heat. Even the birds sat quietly in the trees, trying to stay cool. Out on Scott Road, in front of the Barnhards' house, a herd of scrawny Indian cows strolled along, nibbling on the roadside weeds. Behind them wandered a little herd-boy, who had only enough energy to wave his stick at the cows now and then. Somewhere in the distance a bell tinkled, announcing the progress of the ice cream man as he pedaled his cart down the road.

Con, seated on the piano bench, was practicing his scales. At least, that's what it *looked* like he was doing. His fingers were mechanically running up and down the keys, producing a fine-sounding C-scale. But a comic book was propped up where his music should have been. He had checked it out of the Penang library when they had gone with the Perkinses the week before. Con was deep into the adventures of Jaydee, Captain Bluebeard, and their dog Skeeter, who had bumped into some crooks during a deep-sea fishing expedition.

"Conrad!" Addie's irritated yell from the dining room broke his concentration.

Con stopped playing. "What?"

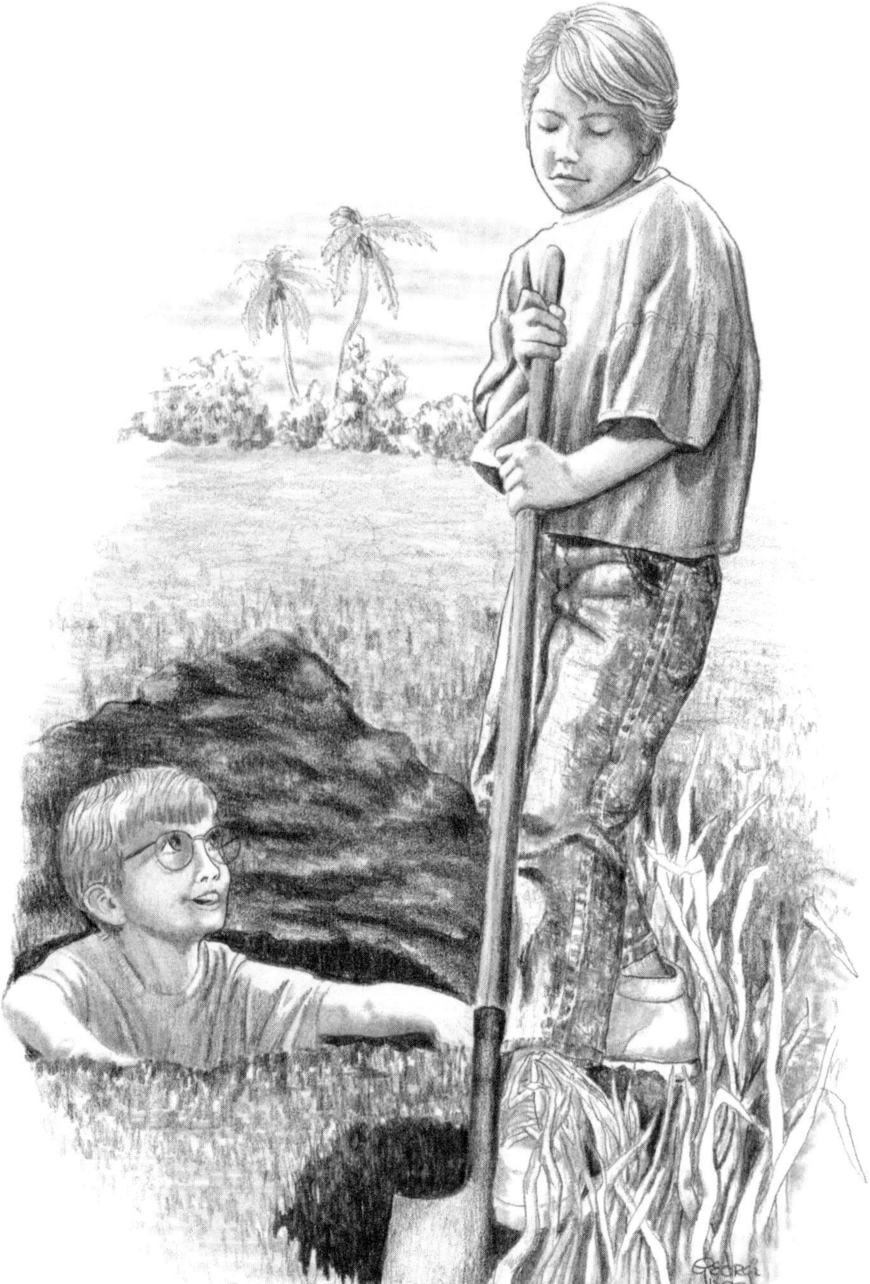

THE UNDERGROUND HIDEOUT

"I'm sick of hearing that same scale over and over. Can't you play something else?"

"OK," said Con, and he began playing a scale in the key of G instead. Addie's groan came loud and clear from the other room. "Well, you said to play something else," called Con. "This is a different scale."

"*I meant* that you should play a song!" said Addie, coming into the living room. She noticed the comic book propped against the music stand. "Hey, that's not fair! You're supposed to be practicing. You can't count time for reading comics."

"I'm practicing my scales," Con replied defensively. "If I can read and practice at the same time, why shouldn't I?"

Mercifully for Con, the telephone rang just then, cutting off any more of his sister's bossy displeasure. Addie ran to answer the phone.

"Hello.... Hi, Nathan.... No, we don't have anything planned for today.... Sure, we can come over. Con's doing his practicing, so we'll come in a while. OK, thanks. 'Bye."

"Are we going over to the Perkins's house?" Con asked.

"Yeah," said Addie. "Nathan said they're playing cricket this afternoon with their dad when he gets home from work."

"OK," said Con. "I'll be finished with my practicing in ten more minutes." He settled back at the piano, eyes glued to the comic book, fingers running up and down on the G-scale. Addie sighed and rolled her eyes. It was useless to try to make Con do it right. She could always tattle to Mama later, she decided.

Fifteen minutes later the children let themselves out the back gate of the hospital compound. Soon they were

45

THE FIERY DRAGON GANG

pedaling up Brown Road toward the Perkins's house. The road was lined with flame-of-the-forest trees, which were in full bloom. The branches of flaming red-orange blossoms stretched over the road. Now and then a bright petal drifted down.

Pulling up at the Perkins's gate, Addie and Con got off their bikes. Con undid the gate bolt, and they walked through the gate toward the old gray English-style bungalow set back from the road. A spacious green lawn surrounded the house. From the middle of the lawn rose a gigantic African tulip tree. African tulip buds made great natural water pistols. You could pinch one of them, and water would squirt out from the inside. By the front hedge stood some ixora plants. Addie pulled off one little flower as she went by the bushes. She stuck the stem in her mouth and sucked. A little taste of sweetness settled on her tongue.

The Barnhard children parked their bikes under the kitchen window and walked around to the back door of the Perkins's house. They knocked and slipped their thongs off before entering.

"Hello." The Perkins's housemaid, Rosa, appeared from the front room wearing her usual simple blouse and wraparound sarong. "You looking for Nathan and Paul and Joel? They are in the back," she informed the children.

"Thanks, Rosa." Addie and Con headed for the backyard, behind the garage and servants' quarters.

The Perkins's house was built in the English style, with the main house in front and a long addition built on the back at a ninety-degree angle to the house. The addition was made up of five or six rooms for storage and servants' quarters. Since Rosa lived in a housing development near the Chinese cemetery, the Perkins family used the servant rooms mostly for storage. At the end of the servants' quarters was the garage, and behind it a large washing area. It was meant for doing laundry and charcoal cooking in the old-fashioned Chinese way. It had walls, but no roof on it. Since the Perkinses owned a washing machine, they didn't use the washing area. This was where Con and Addie found the Perkins boys.

"Hullo!" The three Perkins boys rounded the corner of the washroom.

"Hi," said Con. "What's happening?"

"Nathan jumped off the roof this morning," said Paul, squinting at Addie and Con to see how they would react to such a feat of daring.

"No way!" Addie exclaimed. "That's too high to jump off."

"I did too!" said Nathan proudly. "I jumped off the roof of the servants' quarters, didn't I, boys?"

"Yeah," chorused Paul and Joel.

"Well, then, let's see you do it again!" dared Con.

"All right," said Nathan, lifting his chin. He shinned up the drainpipe on the back of the servants' quarters and perched on the edge of the roof.

Addie shaded her eyes as she looked up at Nathan. "Nathan, don't do it," she warned, feeling a tingle of worry in her chest. "It looks pretty dangerous." Con, Paul, and Joel stood watching with great anticipation written across their faces.

"Watch this," said Nathan. He dropped from the roof, landing on his feet and breaking his fall by rolling over on the ground.

"Wow!" said Con. "That's pretty good."

"Con, don't you try it," Addie warned.

"Oh, I wasn't going to. Not unless I have an umbrella, anyway. An umbrella could work like a parachute."

THE FIERY DRAGON GANG

"Hey, yeah," said Joel. "That's how Mary Poppins flies, with an umbrella."

"Mary Poppins isn't real, Joel," said Addie disdainfully. "Don't you know that?"

"Of course he knows that," said Paul, defending his little brother. "Anyhow, we should get an umbrella sometime and try it."

"Well, I don't know," Con said doubtfully, having thought the idea over. "I suppose you could poke your eye out if one of the spokes hit you in the face. Maybe we'd better not." Con's words made sense. The children decided to scrap the umbrella idea. They sat down on the edge of the walkway between the house and the servants' quarters with their elbows on their knees, chins resting on their hands.

"So what are we going to do now?" asked Addie. The children looked at Nathan expectantly. He could usually be counted on to come up with an idea.

"Well, Dad's not home from the hospital yet, so we can't play cricket," said Nathan. Addie breathed a sigh of relief. She never understood the rules for cricket, even though Nathan had tried to explain them several times. "You know, I was thinking," Nathan continued, "that we should have another clubhouse. We should have one here as well as on the hospital compound."

"Why?" asked Addie.

"Because we play over here a lot," said Nathan, "and sometimes Jerry is over here, and it would be fun to disappear where he couldn't find us."

"Where would we put it?" asked Paul. "You can't really hide anything in our yard."

"It would be nice to have a cave, like the Daring Detectives had in the Marcia Green books," suggested Addie. "They slept in their cave and kept food there and stuff."

THE UNDERGROUND HIDEOUT

"Well, there aren't any caves close by here," Con pointed out.

"True," said Nathan. "But we might *dig* one. Like an underground room." The other children all turned and stared at him.

"What do you mean, 'underground room'?" asked Paul.

"Just what I say," Nathan said impatiently. "An underground room. We could dig it somewhere and have a tunnel that leads into it."

"That sounds like a good idea!" Addie was enthusiastic. "It shouldn't take that long with all of us working on it!"

"Well, what are we waiting for?" Nathan asked. "Where shall we start digging?"

"What about back there?" Paul pointed to a cluster of banana trees in the corner of the Perkins's backyard. Behind the fence was a grove of rambutan trees. The children jumped up and ran over to inspect the corner.

"Yeah, this looks like a good place," said Nathan. "No one comes back here except the cats. We could carry on without being disturbed here."

"I'll get the shovel," said Joel. He took off toward the garage, where the gardener kept his tools.

"Get any spades you see as well," Con called after him.

Soon the children had marked off a round spot in the gray clay for their tunnel. With a great deal of energy they began to dig. There weren't enough spades for everyone, so Addie helped out by emptying the buckets of dirt under the banana trees. Joel, being the smallest, just stood around and watched.

"It's a shame we haven't more spades," puffed Nathan. Sweat poured down his face and dripped off his jaw as he dug with the shovel. His wet hair clung to his forehead. "Once we get down a ways, one of us can dig, and

THE FIERY DRAGON GANG

the other ones will have to empty the buckets. The hole is going to be too small to fit more than one person in here."

"How are we going to hide this tunnel?" asked Con. "Jerry might come over here to play sometime, and he'd see it."

"We can camouflage it," said Nathan wisely. "You know, the way jungle soldiers do. We can cover it with leaves off the banana trees."

"Oh," said Con, who was not as well read on the ways of jungle soldiers.

"Hey, you know what?" Addie exclaimed as she surveyed the back corner of the yard. "If we have our underground room just here," she stepped out the size on the ground, "it would probably go under the fence as well. We could have an emergency escape hatch coming out in the rambutan grove back there." Addie pointed across the fence at the grove. "That way if Jerry came and found our entrance, we could climb out the back and run away."

"Good idea," said Con, his face lighting up. "And we could have tunnels down there, and a place where we could store tins of food and crackers."

The children chattered happily about their plans of tunnels and hidden food as they dug. But after a while, they ran out of things to plan. It was terribly hot. Their hole hadn't gotten very deep yet. The dirt was awfully hard packed—it seemed like they were hacking at cement to dig their hole. The children lapsed into silence as they dug and emptied buckets. It seemed like hours had passed when Bah Chee, the gardener, came around the corner. He stopped short at the sight of the children digging away.

"What you are doing?" Bah Chee asked in typical Ma-

THE UNDERGROUND HIDEOUT

laysian-style English.

"We're digging a tunnel," replied Nathan. "Do you have any more spades or shovels?"

"No," said Bah Chee. "Why you are digging a tunnel?"

"So we can hide," said Paul, taking off his thick glasses and using his shirt to wipe his sweaty face.

"Paul!" Nathan warned. The others remembered that this was supposed to be a *secret* tunnel and underground room. Paul, silenced by Nathan's warning, stood nervously on one foot. He scratched his leg with the side of the other foot, leaving a muddy streak where he scratched.

Bah Chee inspected the scene. Nathan stood waist deep in the hole. Little piles of dirt surrounded the banana trees in the corner of the yard behind the hole. The Perkins's cats nosed around the dirt piles, pawing at them and sniffing daintily. Joel, tired of standing in the sun, sat on the back walkway of the servants' quarters with his chin in his hands, watching the other children. Bah Chee's lips twitched as if he wanted to smile. "Good luck," he commented. "You be careful." He walked away toward the rambutan trees on the other side of the house to sweep up the fallen leaves from the grass.

Nathan stood with his hands on his hips, watching Bah Chee go. He wiped his forehead with the back of his hand, leaving a gray smear across his forehead. "Well," he sighed, "I'm too hot and tired to work on this anymore." The other children nodded. Digging an underground room had turned out to be much harder work than they had imagined. "Let's go get a drink and play inside," Nathan suggested. He hopped out of the hole, covered it up with a few banana leaves, and went to wash himself off at the hose. The other children followed.

51

THE FIERY DRAGON GANG

"We can work on this another day," said Addie, as much to herself as to the others. "This might take a while to finish."

"Yeah," agreed Nathan. "Maybe next time we'll need to soften up the ground first with water or something. But I don't want to work on it anymore today."

Having washed off, the children trooped into the house for some cool juice. They drank it while sitting under the ceiling fan, which they had turned up to the "high" setting. It felt wonderful to rest. "Maybe another day," Addie promised herself. "Another day we'll finish the job. But right now this feels sooooo good!"

6
Seven-Up's Ladder

Behind the mission hospital on the compound where the Barnhards lived stood the maintenance building. The missionary children called it "the workshop." At least five or six Chinese men worked there, repairing hospital equipment, building cabinets, and moving heavy things for the hospital. They also did any repainting or odd jobs that were needed around the compound.

Addie loved to drop in and watch the workshop men as they sawed and sanded and varnished. One of the most interesting tools to watch was the electric plane. The workshop man would line up a piece of wood and run it along the guidepiece on a flat metal table with a kind of whirling wheel in it that straightened and smoothed the wood. Below the machine a huge cone-shaped pile of sawdust rose higher every day from all the pieces of wood that had been planed. Addie loved to stroke the smooth boards that had been across the machine. They felt like cool silk to her touch. The sweet, spicy smell of tropical woods filled the workshop. In the sunlight that streamed in the eastern doorway of the workshop, little dust and wood particles rose and fell on the sunbeams, puffing around now and then when the breeze brushed by them.

Addie's best friend at the workshop was Wah Seng,

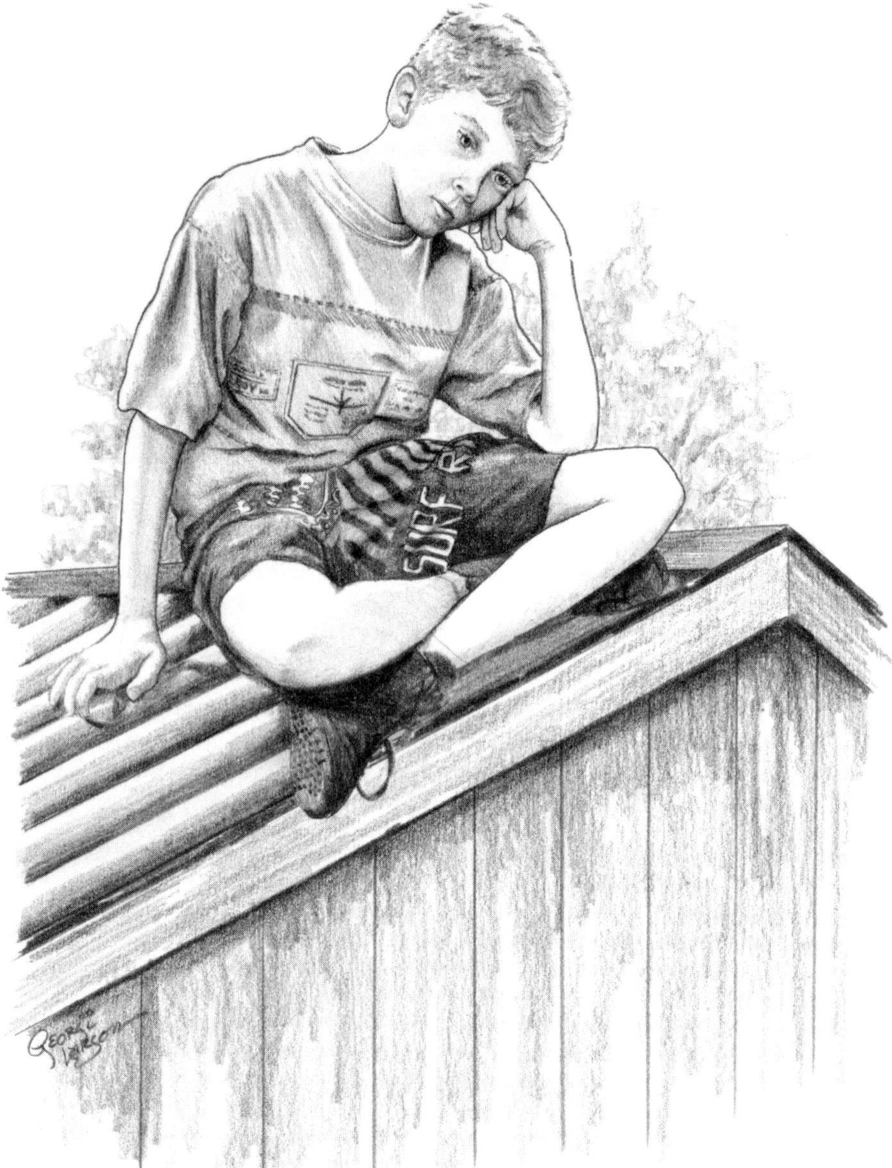
SURF

SEVEN-UP'S LADDER

the supervisor. He spoke English and was always very friendly and helpful. Addie didn't know the names of the other men, though she saw them all the time. They were friendly to the children, talking with signs and gestures, since they didn't know English. Nathan had named the shortest man in the workshop "Seven-Up." He had come up with the name one time because Seven-Up had tried to say the English name "Steven," and all he came out with was "Seven." Nathan thought this was hilarious and began calling the nice little man "Seven-Up." The missionary children picked up on the name, and soon even their parents called the little man "Seven-Up."

One afternoon, as the children were sitting in school, they heard the shuffling, flappy sound of slippers coming up the path toward the school. Looking out, Addie saw Seven-Up carrying a tall wooden ladder up the pathway. Paul, curious as always, jumped up from his desk and ran to the door to see what Seven-Up might be planning to do with the ladder.

"Paul," called Miss Vanden from her desk, "you need to get back to work." She glanced at her watch and added, "Oh, never mind. It's time for recess anyhow."

The children dashed for the door and gathered outside, watching Seven-Up set up the ladder against the side of the school building. The ladder was so tall it reached right up to the reddish shingles on the roof.

"Seven-Up, what you doing?" asked Nathan, trying to use simple English. Seven-Up just grinned his big one-tooth-missing smile and started up the ladder. It swayed and bounced a little as he climbed it.

"I think," said Miss Vanden, "that he is going to clean the leaves out of the rain gutter. They have been blocking it and making the rain pour off the roof where it's

THE FIERY DRAGON GANG

not supposed to. I asked Wah Seng to send someone to fix it."

"Oh," Addie said. She was losing interest in watching Seven-Up's job. The workshop men had to clean out the leaves every now and then, and it wasn't that exciting. "Let's go play," she suggested to the others.

"Freeze tag," yelled Con. "Beat you to the field!" The children raced up the road to the lawn where they usually played their games at recess.

When the children came in from recess, Seven-Up had cleared the rain gutter on the back of the school roof, and he still had the front one to do. Shortly after he started on the front gutter, one of the other workshop men came by and called Seven-Up away to do something else. He climbed down and left the ladder leaning against the school.

The children noticed the ladder as they left school that afternoon. "I wonder if Seven-Up is going to come back and get his ladder?" Nathan commented, gazing toward the top of the ladder.

"I suppose he'll come back later," replied Addie.

"Come on, you guys," coaxed Con. "Let's go climb trees."

"Yeah," Jerry Norton chimed in.

The other children looked at him, and then at each other. Nathan looked almost as if he were going to tell Jerry to leave. But then he surprised Addie by saying, "Come on, then. What are we waiting for?"

The children headed for their favorite climbing tree near the Barnhards' back pathway. The trunk of the tall tree was forked at the bottom, so that two trunks rose up from the base. They stayed parallel to each other at first, but grew wider apart toward the top. To climb the tree, the children had to brace one leg against one trunk and

SEVEN-UP'S LADDER

one against the other. Wrapping an arm around each trunk and using a knee as a brace now and then, it was possible to inch one's way up to the lowest branches. From there on up the climb was easy, since the branches grew fairly close together all the way up the trunk.

Addie scrambled up about five branches from the first one. Then she looked down and saw how far away the ground was, so she didn't go up any farther. The boys always climbed higher than Addie did. Con always got the highest, climbing up near the top where the tree would sway back and forth in the breeze with his weight.

"Con, be careful," Addie warned, feeling anxious about her brother's being up so high.

"Oh, it's fine up here, Addie," Con called down. "See?" He shook the tree from where he was so that all the branches and leaves shivered.

"Con!" A note of fear entered Addie's tone of voice.

"Don't be so scared, Addie. It's great up here. I can see the mansion on the other side of the laundry," Con commented, gazing toward the big Chinese bungalow on the other side of the jungle lot.

"Yeah, and I can see the Radio Malaysia building across the road from the hospital," added Paul from just below Con.

Feeling nervous in the swaying tree, Addie flattened herself tightly against the trunk and worked her way down a few branches. She felt safer there and swung around the trunk, waiting for the boys to climb back down.

As she waited, Addie saw Miss Vanden riding her bicycle down the road and waved to her. Miss Vanden lived close to the hospital, and she rode her bicycle to the school every day. She sat very straight on the bicycle seat, with her skirt billowing out around her legs as she rode.

THE FIERY DRAGON GANG

After a while the children had explored the tree as much as they wanted to. One by one they climbed down.

"What can we do now?" asked Jerry, standing under the climbing tree and looking expectantly at Nathan.

"I dunno," said Nathan. He stood with his hands on his hips, looking around as though he would find an idea somewhere around him. His gaze stopped as his eyes lighted on the schoolhouse. Seven-Up's ladder still leaned against it. "I say!" Nathan exclaimed. "Seven-Up's left his ladder up against the school. Come along!"

The children took off running for the school. Nathan was the first one there. He scrambled up the ladder to the school roof. It was a little hard to climb the ladder since the rungs were nailed on quite far apart from each other.

"Nathan, I'm coming next," Paul called up to his brother. He started up the ladder. Nathan was gingerly stepping up the slanting roof as his brother started up the ladder.

Addie looked up at the boys above her. She climbed up one or two rungs of the ladder. It felt terribly shaky. "Hey, you guys," she called. "Be careful up there." She climbed back down and backed away from the wall of the building so she could see the boys up on the roof. They were walking around, calling to each other and gloating over their new adventure.

"Come on up, Addie," called Con, walking toward the edge of the roof to look down.

"Con, don't get so close to the edge!" Addie yelled.

"I won't fall," Con sniffed. He turned around and climbed back up the roof.

After a while Con climbed down the ladder, with Paul and Nathan following. Jerry Norton was the last one on top, and he still had to climb over from the other side of

SEVEN-UP'S LADDER

the school roof in order to get down Seven-Up's ladder.

Nathan stood looking up at the roof, waiting for Jerry. Suddenly he turned around and hissed, "Hey, you guys, help me take the ladder away so Jerry can't get down. We'll play a trick on him." Without stopping to think, Con, Paul, and Addie quickly grabbed a hold of the ladder, lifting it away from the roof. As they straightened up from laying it down on the ground, Jerry stepped over to where the ladder was supposed to be.

"Hey, put the ladder back up," Jerry called.

"No," said Nathan. "We're going to leave you up there."

"Why?" asked Jerry with a whiny, scared note in his voice.

"Because," said Nathan. "We don't like you. We'll let you down when we're ready." He started to walk away, beckoning the other children to follow him. Addie hesitated for a moment. It was true, Jerry was sometimes mean to the other children and hard to get along with, and she didn't mind playing a trick on him. But it didn't seem quite right to walk away and leave him there. Addie looked up at Jerry, and then the other direction at Nathan and the others walking away. Nathan turned around. "Come on, Addie!" he hissed. "We'll come back in a little bit. Don't worry."

Making a quick decision, Addie turned and ran to join Nathan, Paul, and Con. "What if he tries to jump or something and breaks his leg?" she asked Nathan.

"He wouldn't be that foolish," said Nathan. "The school roof is too high to jump down from."

"We could just go around the Watsons' house and hide behind their backyard hedge and spy on Jerry for a few minutes," suggested Paul. "Then we'll go let him down."

"OK," said Addie, feeling relieved. That sounded like a

THE FIERY DRAGON GANG

good plan. The children circled around the Watsons' house and crept past the servants' quarters to the backyard hedge. From there it was only a few feet to the road that ran past the schoolhouse. They could peer through the hedge without anyone else seeing them.

Jerry sat up on the roof where they had left him, looking distressed. But he just sat there and didn't do anything. "He really can't do much," thought Addie. "He'll just have to wait." After watching for a few minutes, the children became bored. Their trick seemed pretty funny at first, but now Addie felt restless.

"Let's go put the ladder back," Addie whispered.

"Uh-oh," muttered Con suddenly, pointing through the hedge toward the hospital. Up the path from the hospital came Dr. Norton, on his way home from work.

"We don't have time to get Jerry down. Let's just watch," whispered Nathan.

Addie felt more and more uncomfortable about what might happen as Dr. Norton got closer to the school.

Then Jerry saw his dad. "Dad!" he yelped in a soft, squeaky voice.

Dr. Norton looked up and saw his son perched on the edge of the school roof. He stopped still in his tracks. Dr. Norton's face went reddish purple. "Jerry!" he bellowed. "What on *earth* are you doing up there! Come down this instant!"

"I can't! The ladder is down there. The other kids took it away." Jerry's voice was squeakier than before as he pointed over the edge of the roof to the ladder.

Dr. Norton walked over to the ladder, picked it up, and propped it against the school roof. As Jerry climbed down, his father gave him a tongue-lashing about the dangers of climbing ladders to the roofs of buildings, about thinking before doing silly things, and about letting others trick a person into a bad situation. "And for doing something so foolish, you will stay in the house the rest of the day and not play outside," Dr. Norton finished. Putting his hand on his son's shoulder, he walked Jerry off toward their house.

The children looked at one another without a word, shrinking down behind the bushes in hopes that Dr. Norton wouldn't see them.

"Well, that was something," commented Nathan.

"He really got in trouble," said Paul.

"It wasn't really his fault," Addie said.

"Yeah, but still, I don't feel sorry for him," Nathan responded.

"But maybe we should have let him down sooner," offered Con.

"Well, I don't feel one bit sorry," Nathan repeated. Paul nodded his head in agreement.

Addie wasn't sure how to reply to that, so she left things as they were and kept her mouth shut. She shoved her guilt aside as the children headed for the Barnhards' house to find something else to do.

7
April Fools' Pranks

It would soon be April, and one day the children realized that April Fools' Day was coming. Addie thought of it after school, when Nathan had called a Fiery Dragon Gang meeting at the Barnhards' house.

"It's going to be April Fools' Day next week," said Addie. "Do you celebrate April Fools' Day in Australia?"

"Of course we do," said Paul disdainfully. "Don't you know where April Fools' comes from?"

"No," replied Addie. "Do you?"

"It came from France," said Paul. "When they started using the Gregorian calendar, they changed New Year's from April 1 to January 1. Some people didn't want to change, and they called them 'April Fools' and played tricks on them."

"Oh," said Addie, feeling a little foolish that Paul knew more than she did about the day. After all, she was older than Paul, so she should know more. But Paul's dad was always quizzing his boys on history, so they often came up with interesting bits of information that Addie and Con didn't know.

"We celebrated Guy Fawkes' Day when we were in England," said Nathan. "That was jolly good fun. Fireworks and burning effigies and stuff like that."

"What's an effigy?" asked Con.

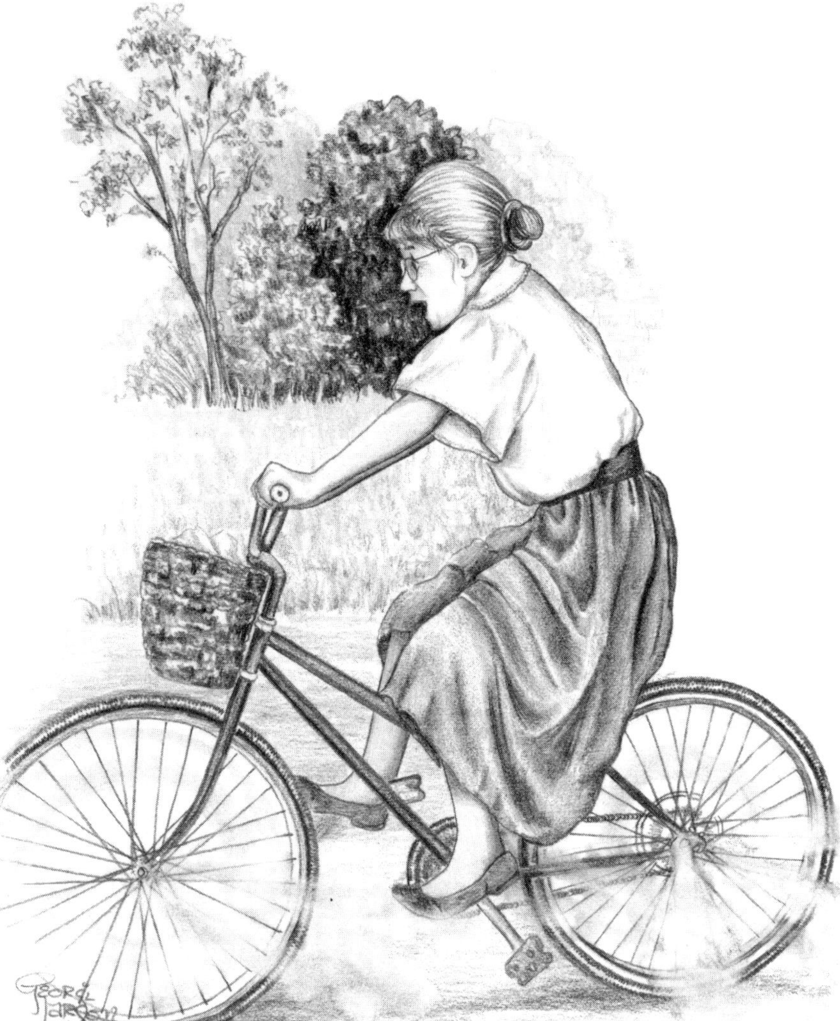

THE FIERY DRAGON GANG

"It's a life-sized puppet," said Nathan. "They get all this hay and dress it in clothes to represent Guy Fawkes, who tried to blow up the king and the parliament. Then they burn it in the nighttime, and it makes a lovely bonfire."

"That sounds fun," said Addie, imagining a bale of hay with clothes on it, going up in flames.

"It sure is," said Paul. "It's better than any holiday you Americans have. Even better than April Fools' Day."

"Well, it's April Fools' Day that's coming up," said Addie impatiently, "so what are we going to do about it? I want to play tricks on somebody."

"What kind of tricks?" asked Con. He thought a minute. "I know! I have some itching powder at home that I got from the market. And I have some sneezing powder and some stink bombs."

"Yuck! Stink bombs!" Addie wrinkled up her nose, thinking of the horrible, rotten-egg smell that poured out of the little glass vials when they were crushed. She looked at Nathan and Paul. They wore delighted looks on their faces at the thought of all Con's treasure, just waiting to be used on some unsuspecting victim.

"We could dust some itching powder down the back of Jerry Norton's shirt," said Paul, grinning. He looked as if he'd like to do the job himself.

"Or get some sneezing powder on him somewhere," said Nathan.

"He doesn't even know there are such things as sneezing powder and itching powder," Paul added. "He won't know what's happened to him!"

"How about the stink bombs?" asked Addie. "Are we going to use those?"

"It would be fun to set off a stink bomb under Miss Vanden's desk," said Nathan.

APRIL FOOLS' PRANKS

"But she might get mad at us," Con cautioned.

"Yeah. Maybe we should save that for some other time," Nathan said.

"I know! We have some Chinese firecrackers at home. How could we use those?" Paul said.

Addie's face brightened. "I have an idea! We could tie them to Miss Vanden's bicycle!"

"Yeah!" Paul exclaimed. "When she rides home they'll get pulled, and then they'll bang and startle her."

The children all laughed at the picture Paul's words made in their minds. They liked their teacher. But she was a lady who meant business, and it might be a little scary to pull a trick on her for April Fools' Day. The "danger" involved made the prank seem all the more inviting.

During the next week, the Fiery Dragon Gang discussed April Fools' Day off and on. They decided that they would tie the Chinese firecrackers to Miss Vanden's bike after school while she was busy grading workbooks. They would also bring some sneezing powder and figure out how to get it near Jerry Norton's nose during the day. Con volunteered his itching powder, and the children decided he should bring it, just in case they wanted to use it on someone.

Nathan arrived at school on April 1 with the firecrackers in his pocket. He had bought them at the roadside market during Chinese New Year a few months before. The children sent each other knowing glances all through the day at school.

At recess time, Nathan sidled up to Jerry as the children walked to the play field. "Hi, Jerry," Nathan said cheerfully.

"Hullo," said Jerry.

"How are you feeling today?" Nathan asked.

THE FIERY DRAGON GANG

"Fine," Jerry replied, looking suspicious at Nathan's sudden concern for his health.

"Sure you're not getting a cold or something?" Nathan persisted.

"No. Why?" Jerry asked, quite curious by now.

"Well, you seem to be sneezing a bit today." Nathan's voice raised in pitch as he reached out and swiped the sneezing powder at Jerry's nose. Jerry ducked as he saw Nathan's arm coming at him, and the sneezing powder got smeared across his cheek. The other children, laughing, watched to see if Jerry would have a sneezing fit. After all, they had never tried sneezing powder before to see if it worked.

Jerry, angry at Nathan's trick, turned beet red, snorted a few times, and wiped the sneezing powder off the side of his face with his hand. "What did you put on me?" he asked, furious at the laughter around him. He sneezed once or twice and turned to Addie. "Is there something on my face?"

"Nothing that shows," Addie replied, still grinning but feeling a little sorry for him. "It's just a bit of sneezing powder."

"A bit of what?" Jerry asked, as though his ears had fooled him.

"Sneezing powder, Jerry. Sneezing powder," said Nathan, laughing. "Haven't you ever heard of it before?"

Jerry, not saying anything more, looked hurt. He ran ahead of them to the playground and sat on a swing by himself, his head hanging.

Addie felt sorry that Jerry had taken their joke that way. When she became team captain for one of the soccer teams, she chose Jerry first. She hoped that would help him feel better. Soon their prank was forgotten in the heat of the game.

APRIL FOOLS' PRANKS

As soon as the closing prayer was over that afternoon and Miss Vanden had dismissed the children from school, work got underway. The children could hardly wait for the crowning event of the day—the firecracker trick on Miss Vanden. The Fiery Dragon Gang children, plus Jerry and his sister, gathered under the rambutan tree beside the school. Since the children couldn't very well pull their prank without Jerry seeing it, they decided to include him in on it. Besides, they couldn't risk Jerry's running to tell Miss Vanden.

Miss Vanden always parked her bike in the shade under the rambutan tree. Nathan fished the firecrackers out of his pocket, dropped them on the ground, and squatted by the back tire of the bike. Paul guarded the school door to make sure Miss Vanden was busy grading workbooks and wouldn't come out to investigate.

"Let's see," said Nathan. "I've got to find something here to tie both ends of each firecracker to."

"Here," suggested Con, "tie one end to a spoke here, and the other end to this." He pointed to the bar that held the rear mudguard in place. Nathan tied the firecracker on the bike. Addie tied another one on the other side. Then they moved to the front tire and tied two more firecrackers there. Tying on the firecrackers took a while, because the strings weren't very long, and it was hard to get them in a knot. At last they finished the job.

"OK, Paul," Addie whispered loudly. Paul still stood at his post by the school door. The children ran behind the Nortons' house, where they felt safe from Miss Vanden's watchful eyes.

"Now what?" asked Jerry.

"Now we just have to wait until Miss Vanden goes home," announced Nathan.

THE FIERY DRAGON GANG

"Well, we can't just wait here," Paul said. "That would be boring."

"What's the best place to play where we can still see Miss Vanden leave?" Nathan asked.

"I know!" Addie exclaimed. "How about going and climbing the tree by our back pathway? We do that all the time, so Miss Vanden wouldn't be suspicious. Then when she leaves, we'll stay hidden up in the tree and watch her go riding by!"

"You mean, 'Watch her go banging and popping by,'" Con commented with a laugh. The children joined in the laughter, imagining the scene in their minds. They took off in a herd for their favorite climbing tree by the Barnhards' back pathway. Soon the boys were high in the tree, swaying back and forth as usual. Addie clung to the lower branches, swinging around the trunk now and then as she held on tightly. Up above her, Nathan hung upside down from a branch. Addie shuddered, thinking how nauseated she would feel if she were in Nathan's place.

The children were so busy playing and talking, they forgot about Miss Vanden and her bicycle. Then they heard the clinking of the louvred glass windows shutting from over at the school. Miss Vanden was preparing to leave! The boys scrambled lower in the tree, where they could see better.

The children, eyes trained on the doorway, saw the ceiling fan inside slow down and stop. Then there was a long silence.

"What's she doing?" Paul asked impatiently.

"She must have found something else to do before she leaves," said Addie.

After a few minutes, Miss Vanden came to the door and stepped outside. She closed and locked the door. Then she stopped to look at the flowers in the flower bed

APRIL FOOLS' PRANKS

that bordered the sidewalk. She touched a few of them, picking off a dead leaf or flower here and there.

"Come *on*, Miss Vanden!" Con whispered impatiently, voicing the feelings of the others.

Finally Miss Vanden walked to her bike, kicked up the kickstand, and wheeled it over to the sidewalk. She got on the bike, arranging her skirt as she settled on the bike seat. After backpedaling to get the pedal in place to go, she took off.

Halfway down the sidewalk, the first firecracker went off. *Pop!* The children, perched in the tree, saw Miss Vanden leap off her seat in surprise. Landing beside her bicycle, she bent down to inspect the tires.

"She thinks a tire blew out!" Paul whispered between giggles. All the children had their hands over their mouths, trying to stifle their laughter.

"I hope she doesn't take all the firecrackers off now," Addie whispered back.

As the children hoped, Miss Vanden didn't notice the other firecrackers tied to her bike. She pulled off the strings of the one that had popped, got back on her bike, and started off again. *Pop! Bang! Pop!* The other firecrackers went off, one after another. Miss Vanden, startled at the explosions, wobbled and weaved a little on her bicycle. But she pedaled bravely on down the road and around the corner.

As soon as Miss Vanden was out of sight, the children burst into laughter. "That was so funny!" hooted Nathan. "Did you see how puzzled she looked when she couldn't find a flat tire?" He dissolved into laughter again.

"And did you see her bicycle weave back and forth on the road?" Addie giggled. "She must have been so surprised!"

The next morning the children slunk into school more

THE FIERY DRAGON GANG

quietly than usual. They wondered what Miss Vanden would say to them about the firecracker incident. But Miss Vanden didn't mention it at all. It seemed that she had either forgotten what had happened, or decided to ignore it. Addie, who had been worried about getting punished, felt relieved that the incident would be forgotten.

Partway through the morning, Miss Vanden finished teaching one of the classes and made an announcement. "Children," she began, "it's been a while since you had your last typhoid and cholera shots. It's time for us all to go down to the hospital this morning and get them."

"Oh, no!" the children groaned. They *hated* getting shots, but it was required every three to six months for foreigners living in Malaysia. The shots would protect them from the epidemics that swept through the country now and then.

"Do we *have* to?" Con asked with obvious dismay.

"Yes," said Miss Vanden. "Mrs. Tan talked with me this morning, and you're all to go down to the outpatient nurses' station." She paused. "Come on. Put your books away. If we go right now, we'll be back in time for recess."

The children rose from their desks, pushed their chairs in, and headed for the door. They stopped to put on their thongs, which were lined up on the doorstep. As they crossed the campus toward the hospital, Addie felt tears begin to well up in her eyes. "I *hate* shots!" she thought. "I *hate* it that we have to have shots more often than children in America or Australia. I'm never going to get used to them."

Looking at the faces of the other children, Addie saw that they dreaded the shots as much as she did. One tear rolled down Addie's cheek, and then another.

APRIL FOOLS' PRANKS

The group of children, quieter than usual, entered the outpatient nurses' station through the back door. Miss Vanden followed behind them. Mrs. Tan, the head nurse, bustled up in her starchy white uniform, her pert cap pinned firmly on her black hair. Patients sat on chairs in the waiting room. In one corner a nurse was taking a patient's blood pressure. By the door another nurse adjusted the weights on the scales where her patient stood. Addie could see a foot through the crack of a green curtain pulled around a treatment table. Someone was lying there, waiting for a nurse or doctor. The air was heavy with hospital antiseptic.

"Well, children, are you here for your shots?" Mrs. Tan asked cheerfully. She looked at Miss Vanden and smiled. Something about that smile looked fishy, as if there were something going on between Miss Vanden and Mrs. Tan.

Then Miss Vanden chuckled and said, "April Fools, children!"

Addie, Con, Nathan, Paul, and Jerry just stood there with their mouths open, looking at Miss Vanden. Disbelief crossed their faces.

Mrs. Tan grinned and folded her arms, watching the children's reactions.

"What do you mean, 'April Fools'?" asked Paul, finally finding his tongue.

"I mean April Fools!" repeated Miss Vanden. "I believe it was my turn to pull a trick on you, wasn't it?"

"Ohhhhh," groaned Nathan. "That's not fair!"

"It is *too* fair," said Miss Vanden. "I do believe we're even now!" She turned and thanked Mrs. Tan with a smile, and then nudged the children toward the door. "Come on, now let's go back and have recess."

It was a quiet walk back to school. Addie felt a little

THE FIERY DRAGON GANG

angry at Miss Vanden. After all, getting shots is not something to joke about. Suddenly, Addie realized what it was like to be on the victim's side. April Fools' Day didn't seem quite so much like the funniest day in the year anymore.

8
The Japanese Fort Expedition

"Guess what we did yesterday!" exclaimed Nathan one Monday morning as he stepped in the door of the schoolroom. He was nearly bursting with his news.

"What?" asked Con.

"Tell us," urged Addie.

"We found some World War II Japanese tunnels," said Paul, shoving through the doorway past Nathan.

"Hey, Paul! I was telling them!" Nathan grabbed his brother by the shoulder and shook him rudely.

"OK! OK! You go ahead and tell it then!" Paul gave in to his older brother.

"Well," Nathan began importantly, "yesterday we went with Dad to this village out near the airport. It's called Batu Tanjong. Do you know where it is?"

"No," replied Addie. "Where is it?"

"You turn left before you reach the airport and take the road that goes past the end of the runway. It goes out to Batu Tanjong, right on the beach."

"Oh, I know which road you mean," said Con. "It's the one we fly over when we land at the airport. Addie, you remember. It goes out toward a couple little hills by the ocean."

"Yeah, that's right," Nathan said. "Anyhow, Raju, who

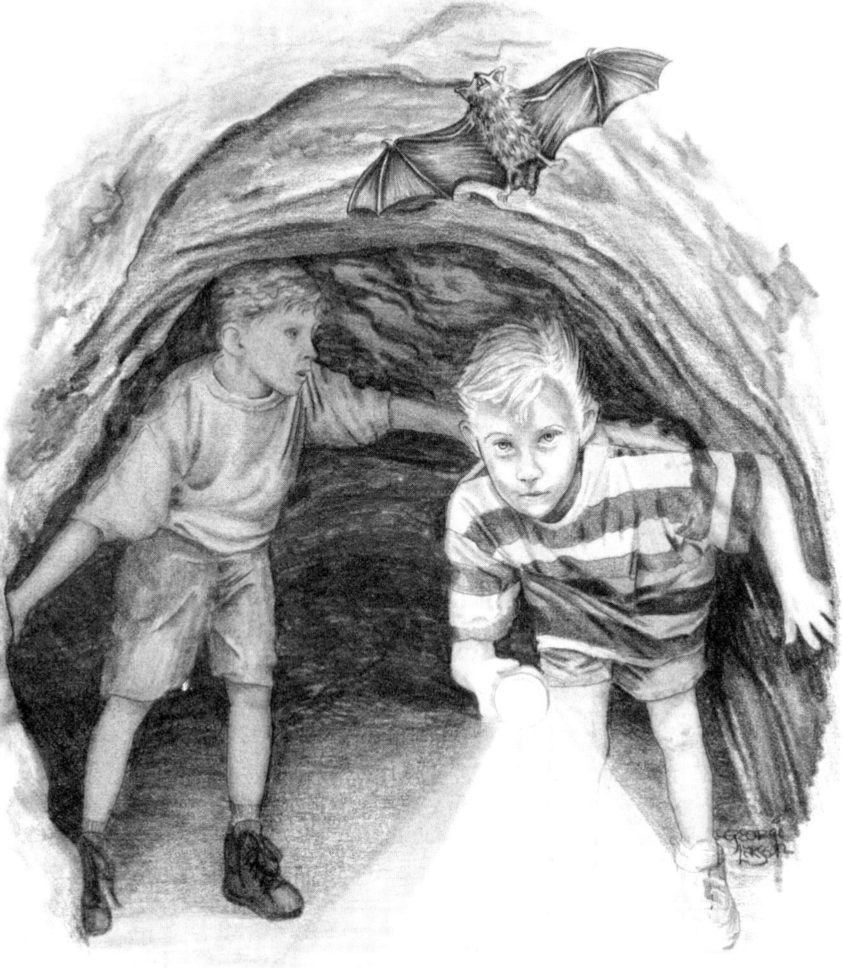

THE JAPANESE FORT EXPEDITION

works at the hospital, told Dad there are some old Japanese tunnels and gun emplacements left there from the war. So we went with him and Dad yesterday to have a look."

"So what did you see there?" asked Con.

"We explored a gun emplacement," Nathan said. "And I found a half-buried shell there from a heavy artillery gun. It's jolly good. I brought it home."

"Wow!" Con breathed admiringly, his eyes growing wide. "What does it look like?"

"Like a big bullet shell, this big," explained Nathan, holding his hands about a foot apart.

"It's kind of rusty, though," said Paul.

"Did you bring it to school with you?" Addie asked.

"No, it's too heavy to bring on my bike," said Nathan. "You can come over and have a look at it, if you like."

"We went in some tunnels too," Paul broke in.

"What kind of tunnels?" asked Con.

"Old Japanese tunnels. They run under the hill so the soldiers could get around if they were under siege," Paul explained. "But we had time to explore only a couple of them. We're going back after Dad's done with morning clinic next Sunday."

"Do you guys want to come?" Nathan asked.

"Yeah!" Con and Addie chorused eagerly. Who in their right mind would turn down an opportunity like that!

"What about me?" asked Jerry. "I want to go explore."

"Sorry, but there's room in our car only for Addie and Con," said Nathan, giving Jerry a pat on the back.

"I never get to do fun things with the rest of you," Jerry complained. "You always leave me out."

"We can't help it that our car only holds a certain number of people," said Nathan, walking away.

Jerry looked at Paul, who shrugged and went to his

75

THE FIERY DRAGON GANG

desk. Addie sighed and sat down in her own chair.

The next Sunday Addie and Con dressed in old clothes that they could get muddy. Nathan had mentioned that exploring was a rather messy business. Knowing that morning clinic would be over at one o'clock, Addie and Con made sure they got their piano practicing done early. The clock seemed to slow down its ticking, and Addie thought the time would never arrive for Dr. Perkins to pick them up.

Finally the Perkins's Toyota pulled up outside. Addie, Con, and Joel sat in the back seat. Nathan and Paul sat in the front seat beside Dr. Perkins.

Dr. Perkins was a tall, very large man, with a booming Australian accent and his own way of saying things. His family, co-workers, and patients all knew that he loved three things: badminton (a game like tennis), durian (a very stinky, spiky green fruit), and historical facts.

"Well, boys—and girl," Dr. Perkins added solicitously, glancing at Addie, "here we go on our great adventure! I have a question for you. Let's see who knows the answer. Who can tell me when the Japanese occupied the tunnels we're going to have a look at?"

There was silence in the car. The children would rather not answer one of Dr. Perkins's questions if they might be wrong.

Finally Nathan ventured, "Was it around 1942, Dad?"

"Right you are, Nathan, my boy!" answered Dr. Perkins proudly. "The Japanese took Penang in 1942. They occupied the whole of Malaya from 1942 until they surrendered to the British in 1945."

"Dad, did they ever have a real battle here in Penang? Did they use the tunnels and the artillery on the hill where we're going?" asked Paul.

THE JAPANESE FORT EXPEDITION

"No, son, they didn't use them in battle," Dr. Perkins replied. He paused as he maneuvered the car around a traffic circle.

"But you see," he continued, "Penang is located in a very strategic place, in the straits of Malacca. It's on the main shipping lane from India to Singapore. It's also between the Indian and Pacific oceans. So the Japanese had to make sure they were fortified here, in case of attack from sea or land."

"How come no one attacked the Japanese here?" Addie asked.

"There was no threat nearby, you see," Dr. Perkins explained. "The British surrendered Singapore to the Japanese in February of 1942. That was a sad, sad day for our brave boys. From 1942 until the end of the war, the Japanese held the whole of Southeast Asia. It was only in the Pacific islands and the Philippines where they lost their battles with the Allies. The Japanese gave up Malaya and Singapore when they surrendered in 1945. That was after atom bombs were dropped on Nagasaki and Hiroshima."

The children rode silently for a while. Addie noticed that they were passing a Japanese bunker. It still sat in the rice fields as a silent testimony to the Japanese occupation so many years before. The massive cement walls were blackened with time and dotted here and there with fungi. Weeds stood tall around the steel door. Through the small square window on the side of the bunker, Addie glimpsed graffiti painted on the inner walls.

Finally Dr. Perkins turned left onto the Batu Tanjong road, and then onto a narrow road that wound up a hill. The Toyota bumped over the potholes. Elephant grass taller than a man flanked both sides of the road. Addie

THE FIERY DRAGON GANG

could see that few people traveled this way. Soon the road narrowed to a one-lane dirt track with weeds sprouting in the center. Dr. Perkins found a wide spot in the road, pulled the car over, and parked.

"Now is the time for all good explorers and adventurers to hop out!" he announced cheerfully. "Come on, boys—and girl!" Seeing Addie's grin, Dr. Perkins added, "Sorry, Addie, for tacking you on. I'm used to having just my boys along."

Addie turned and saw that she'd better hurry to keep up with the others. Nathan and Paul were already running up the track. Addie and Con scrambled to keep up with them. The children took off on a trail leading through the jungle. The trail widened as it crested the hill.

Nathan slowed down and pointed up a rise to the right of the trail. "Up there is the emplacement we explored," he said.

"Let's have another look at it," Paul suggested, clambering up the dirt bank. The others followed. They came out by a large circle of cement lying in the middle of the jungle.

"What's an emplacement, anyway?" asked Addie.

"It's a place that the military prepares for weapons or military equipment," explained Dr. Perkins.

"Are the weapons still here?" Addie asked, looking around the cemented area.

"Do you see any?" Con asked, a little sarcastically.

"No," Addie replied, "but I wouldn't know what they look like, anyway."

"The artillery was here," Nathan said, pointing to a place in the middle of the emplacement where the cement had dips in it. Steel contraptions stuck up from them. "They attached the guns to these," Nathan ex-

THE JAPANESE FORT EXPEDITION

plained to the other children.

"I want to find an artillery shell like Nathan's," said Con, scanning the ground as he walked around.

"We looked a lot last time," said Paul, "and we found only the one Nathan has."

"Dad, I want to go in the tunnels," said Joel, tugging on his father's arm.

"Well, boys—and girl," Dr. Perkins said, nodding at Addie, "shall we go find the tunnels?"

"Yeah!" the children all chorused.

Nathan and Paul went crashing down the hill through the underbrush, with the others following. They came out on a trail. In the trail was a very deep pit made of cemented walls with a rusty steel ladder running down one wall. Addie peered into the hole. Sand, muck, and leaves covered the bottom of the pit. To one side of the bottom was a low doorway.

"Is that a tunnel?" Addie asked. Nathan was already climbing down the ladder.

"We went in this one last week," Paul said as he climbed down the ladder after his brother. "Come on," he called, pausing on the ladder to look up at the others. Con was already turned around, starting down the ladder.

"Are you going?" Addie asked Dr. Perkins. The pit looked so deep, and the entrance to the tunnel at the bottom looked very small. She wondered if Dr. Perkins would fit in the tunnel.

"No," Dr. Perkins said. "Joel and I will stay here till they get back. Nathan," he called down to his oldest son, "we'll wait for you here."

Nathan, just ducking into the tunnel, called back, "OK." He pulled a flashlight out of his pocket, switching it on. Bending over, he disappeared into the dark hole, with Paul and Con right behind him. Addie imagined

79

THE FIERY DRAGON GANG

being in the tunnel with the blackness closing in on her. She moved away from the pit, deciding to stay with Dr. Perkins.

Addie, Joel, and Dr. Perkins sat down on the bank beside the trail and waited. The minutes crawled by. Addie wondered where the boys were. She began to feel sorry that she hadn't ignored her fears and gone with them. They were probably having lots of fun, exploring the tunnels. Who knew what they might be finding? Maybe guns or stuff like that which the Japanese might have left behind when they departed. Or maybe they might stumble across the skeleton of a Japanese soldier. Maybe one had remained behind or gotten lost and died in there. Addie shivered as her imagination made up all kinds of stories.

Dr. Perkins started talking about World War II. He told some stories he had heard from hospital employees who had lived through the Japanese occupation. Addie listened. At the same time, she trained her attention on the pit, waiting to hear the voices of the boys. Were they lost? Maybe there were booby traps or something down there.

Suddenly crashing, crackling noises filtered through the jungle behind them. Addie jumped up and peered through the brush to see who was coming.

"Dad!" came a shout through the jungle. It was Nathan, Paul, and Con! "Dad!" the call came again.

"Right here!" Dr. Perkins called. The boys came stomping out of the jungle, dirty and sweaty. They looked very excited.

"The tunnel comes out on the other side of the hill!" Con exclaimed.

"There were a bunch of turnoffs we didn't explore," Paul added.

THE JAPANESE FORT EXPEDITION

"Did you have to crawl in the tunnel?" Addie asked.

"No, you have to crouch as you walk in some places, but it's not bad," Con reassured his sister. "Come on! It's so much fun exploring in there! And the tunnel comes right out at the side of the hill." He started off back into the jungle. The others followed, including Dr. Perkins.

"Nathan, what did you see in there?" Joel asked, happy that he could go along this time.

"We found a dog skeleton," Nathan announced proudly.

"And Dad, there are bats in there in some places," Paul added.

"Yuck!" Addie exclaimed.

"Are you scared of bats?" Paul asked, grinning.

"No," Addie defended herself. "It's just that I don't like bats flying around my head."

"They won't bump into you," Paul reassured her. "They have sonar."

"What's sonar?" asked Joel.

"It's like radar, Joel," his father explained. "Bats send out signals that bounce back, so they can tell where other objects are. Then they don't bump into things."

The group brushed through the jungle, over fallen tree branches, and through the undergrowth. Soon they started down the other side of the hill. Here the ground became much steeper. Addie clutched at bushes and trees to keep from slipping down the hillside.

"It's right down there," Nathan said, pointing. Through the jungle loomed mossy bunkers set into the hillside. The children reached the doorway of one and stepped inside. They stopped to look at the cement shelves set into the side of the hill.

"These could be either for soldiers to sleep on or for

THE FIERY DRAGON GANG

storing ammunition," suggested Nathan. "What do you think, Dad?"

"I reckon that's a good guess, Nathan," replied Dr. Perkins.

Nathan turned on his flashlight and led the others into the entrance of a tunnel. Addie switched on the flashlight she had brought along. She was glad she had her own light.

The tunnel smelled musty, and it stank. It was big enough to walk in comfortably, even for Dr. Perkins. Decaying leaves covered the floor for the first few feet, probably tracked in by animals. The children followed several turns in the tunnel. Now and then black shadows chirped and flapped past their heads. Bats! Addie cringed and ducked her head.

"Careful." Nathan, at the front of the line, skirted around something on the floor. "Mice nest," he commented. Addie shone her light on it as she walked by. Bits of leaves, grass, and fluffy material rested against the wall in a pile. A mouse skittered past her feet, squeaking shrilly. Addie hurried on as Dr. Perkins and Joel stopped to shine their light on the nest.

The tunnel eventually opened into a small underground room. "Have a look at this," Nathan said, shining his light around the room. His light showed a contraption on one side of the room. It seemed to be a tunnel leading straight up, with light filtering down from an opening at the top. Dr. Perkins came over and examined the contraption.

"What is it, Dad?" Paul asked eagerly.

"Well," Dr. Perkins said slowly, still thinking. "It seems to be a tube that would carry things up to ground level."

"Are we under a gun emplacement?" Nathan asked.

THE JAPANESE FORT EXPEDITION

"Oh, yeah!" Con exclaimed. "They would have to get ammunition up to ground level somehow. This is an elevator to take it up!"

"Con, my boy, I do think you might be right," said Dr. Perkins, peering up toward the light. "The Japanese certainly planned this carefully, didn't they?" he commented.

Nathan, satisfied that they had explored everything in this room, headed for another tunnel entrance. "Come on, let's go," he called back to the others.

The group spent another hour exploring tunnels and the bunkhouses on the side of the hill. Some of the tunnels had low ceilings, and even the children had to bend down to walk through them. All of the rooms they came to were bare, with cement floors, walls, and ceilings. Addie wondered if they would find any Japanese furniture or weapons left from many years before. But she was disappointed. "Probably other people came here before we found it," she thought. "They would have taken anything interesting with them."

Finally Dr. Perkins asked, "Well, gang, are we ready to go?"

"I am," said Addie, who was tired and dirty.

"Aw, Dad, can't we stay a bit longer?" Paul asked.

"Yeah, we haven't seen everything yet," Nathan chimed in.

"I think I have a group of very tired, very dirty children," said Dr. Perkins. "It's getting rather close to dinnertime, so we'd better start off home. Mum's going to wonder what's happened to us."

The group headed for the car, and soon they were on their way home. As they pulled through the gates of the Perkins's yard, Dr. Perkins said, "Well, boys—and girl! Did you all have fun?"

THE FIERY DRAGON GANG

"Yeah!" came the enthusiastic chorus of answers. "Thanks, Dad!" "Thanks, Dr. Perkins!" "Let's go again next week!"

9
Deadwater Rafting

"What are you reading, Nathan?" Con asked one day. He and Addie had just arrived at the Perkins's house to play for the afternoon.

"It's an American book, about this bloke named Huckleberry Finn," said Nathan, looking up from his book. He was sprawled across his bed in the spacious, airy room he shared with his two brothers. "You know, this Huck Finn chap had some jolly good ideas," he commented, waving the book at his friends.

"Yeah? What did he do?" Addie asked.

"You've never heard of Huckleberry Finn?" Nathan asked in surprise. "This book is an American classic!"

"Of course I've heard of him!" Addie retorted. "He was Tom Sawyer's friend. They have Tom Sawyer's island at Disneyland. We were there on our last trip to America."

"Well, you ought to read this book. Huckleberry Finn makes this raft, see, and he gets on it with his friend Jim, and they raft down the Mississippi River and have lots of adventures," Nathan explained.

"Wasn't Huck Finn an orphan?" asked Con.

"Well, he had this dad who was drunk all the time," Nathan said. "But anyhow, I was thinking it would be jolly good fun to make a raft like Huckleberry Finn did."

"Are you going to?" asked Con expectantly.

85

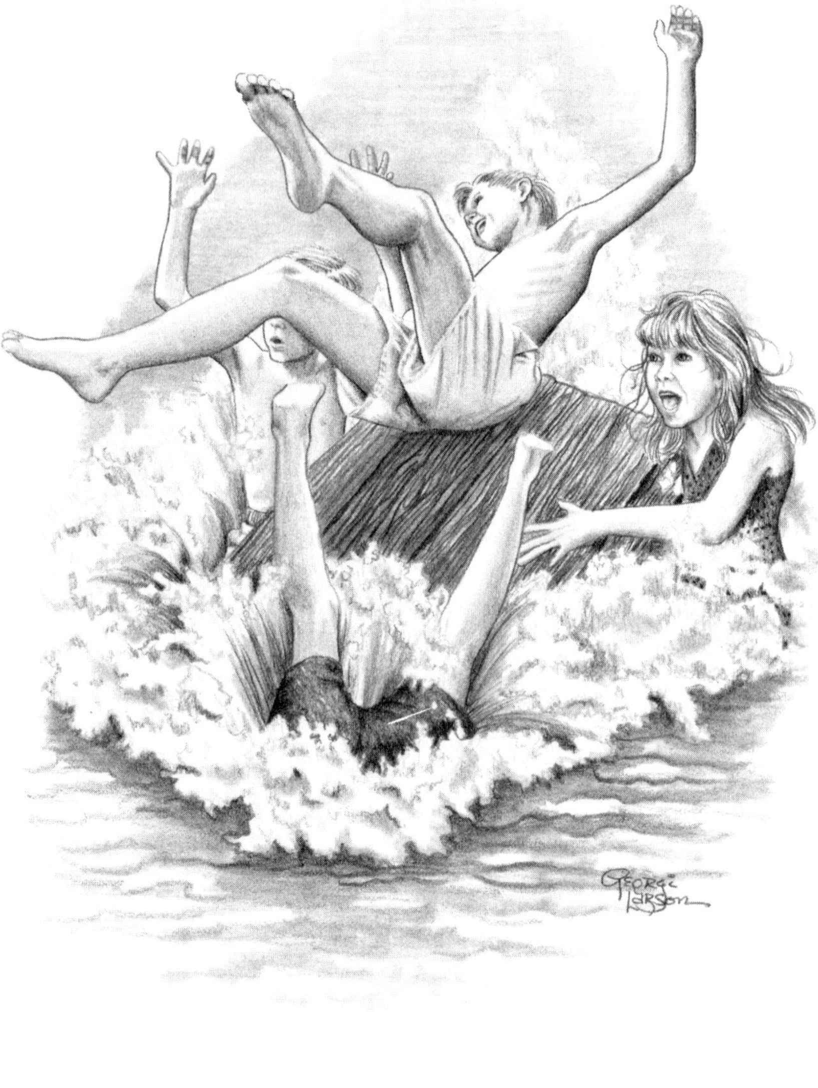
George Larson

DEADWATER RAFTING

"Going to what?" Paul asked, coming into the room with Joel. He had a weird-looking contraption in his hand. Above the handle was a long crosspiece with lenses on one end and a card near the other end. Two prongs stuck out below the lenses. The ends were covered with plastic knobs to keep them from poking a person. On the card was a fancy black cross.

"What is *that*?" Addie asked.

"What is what?" said Paul. "Oh, this?" He held up the contraption. "This is for my eye exercises." He peered at the others through his thick glasses and wrinkled his nose in an effort to push the glasses up higher without using his hands.

"How do you use it?" asked Con.

"Like this." Paul took off his glasses. He held the contraption up so that the knobs were against his cheeks as he looked through the lenses at the card on the other end of the crosspiece. Slowly he moved the card back and forth while peering through the lenses. "That cross on the card is called a Maltese cross," Paul explained.

"And what does that do for you?" Addie asked curiously.

"It's going to strengthen my eyes," replied Paul.

"How?" Addie asked.

"It just does," said Paul. He put his glasses back on and dumped the contraption on his bed. Addie thought Paul's explanation sounded fuzzy, but she figured that was all the information she would get from him.

"So what do you think of making a raft?" asked Nathan, bringing the others back to the subject. "If Huck Finn could make one, so can we."

"A raft! Jolly good idea!" Paul commented enthusiastically.

"Where will we sail it?" asked Joel.

THE FIERY DRAGON GANG

"We could take it to the beach and launch it there," suggested Con.

"Yeah," said Nathan, sounding skeptical. "The waves might be a bit much for it. Let's go see what we have around here for making a raft."

The children hurried out through the living room, dining room, and kitchen. They burst out the swinging back door of the kitchen and stopped.

"We're going to need a hammer and nails," said Nathan. "Paul, go and get those from the garage."

"What about wood?" asked Paul.

Nathan thought for a moment. "I know! We can use that packing crate wood that we play going to heaven on." Nathan led the way past the laundry room and around the back of the house. A pile of boards and packing crates stood in the backyard. Sometimes the gang played a game like king of the mountain, which they called going to heaven. The Bad Guys would try to get the Good Guys off the top of the pile of crates, but of course the Good Guys always won.

Nathan took hold of a square board from the side of a packing crate. They usually used this board as a ramp up to the top of the pile. "Come on! I need some help," he urged the others. Each child grabbed hold of the board, and together they carried it to the breezeway behind the servants' quarters. Paul waited there, having found the hammer and nails.

"How can we make this board float?" asked Addie, looking at it with concern. "If it's this heavy to carry, it can't stay on top of the water."

"We need a flotation device," said Nathan. He sat down on the walkway to think. The others joined him. They all sat in a row, looking through the back fence at the rambutan grove.

DEADWATER RAFTING

"Well, what kind of things float?" Addie asked.
"Styrofoam," suggested Con.
"But where could we get styrofoam?" asked Paul.
"Who knows? What about kapok?" said Addie.
"What's kapok?" Nathan asked.
"It's fluffy stuff from a tree. That's what's inside the life jackets we wear when we go water-skiing. It makes you float."
"I don't know where we could get kapok unless we tie our life jackets underneath the raft," said Con.
"Daddy might not like that," said Addie.
"What we really need is pontoons," said Con.
"Good idea," Nathan said. "We just need to figure out how to make some."
"What are pontoons?" Joel asked.
"They're like hollow tubes under a boat or plane. They hold it up like floaters," explained Con.
"Oh," said Joel, nodding.
"Well, what can we use for pontoons?" Paul asked. "We need something airtight."
"I know! The biscuit tins in the storeroom!" exclaimed Nathan. He jumped up and unlatched the storeroom door beside the breezeway. The others followed him in and picked out four large rectangular biscuit tins. Each had a round lid in the top that had to be pried open with a screwdriver in order to get the tin open. The gang set to work to nail the biscuit tins onto the bottom of their raft. Taking the lid off each tin, they pounded nails into the raft from inside the tins.

Finally, when biscuit tins were in place on each corner of the raft, Nathan pronounced their work done. The gang checked that each lid was securely banged back in place. Then they turned the raft over with the platform side up.

THE FIERY DRAGON GANG

"When are we going to launch it?" Joel asked eagerly. He hopped up on top of the raft to try it out.

"We need our swimming suits," said Addie. "Con and I will have to get ours from home."

"We can't go today, anyhow," Nathan said. "We'll have to wait for one of our parents to take us to the beach."

"I don't think this raft will fit in our car," said Paul.

Nathan squinted at the raft thoughtfully. "I guess it won't," he admitted.

"It would be so much easier if there were somewhere around here to sail it," Addie said.

"We could, you know!" Paul said suddenly. "We could take it to the stream at the end of Brown Road! You know, the Cemetery Stream across Western Road, the one that comes down past the Christian cemetery. We've gone swimming there before."

"Yeah! Jolly good idea, Paul!" exclaimed Nathan, thumping his brother on the back. "We can carry the raft down the road. It's not that far." He turned to Con and Addie. "Can you bring your swimming suits tomorrow after school?"

"Sure!" they replied together.

The next day, after school, as they were leaving for home, Paul said, "Hey, Con, don't forget your swimming suits today."

"What for?" asked Jerry Norton, who hadn't left for his house yet.

"Oh, just something," Paul said lamely.

"Can we come swimming too?" asked Jerry. "Are you going to the swimming club?"

"No, and you can't come this time," Nathan informed him.

"Why not?" Jerry asked.

"Just because, that's why not," replied Nathan.

DEADWATER RAFTING

"You're doing it to me again!" cried Jerry. "You *always* leave me out. You're so mean!" He ran off toward home.

Addie had seen the look on Jerry's face as he turned to go. She ignored it and headed out the school door for home. " 'Bye, Miss Vanden," she called over her shoulder as she ran down the pathway.

Later, at the Perkins's house, Jerry Norton was forgotten as the Fiery Dragon Gang got ready to transport their raft to the Cemetery Stream.

"Each of us will have to carry a corner," Nathan directed the others. "Joel can help on one of the corners since he's the youngest."

The children piled their towels on the raft and found places where they could get a good grip on the raft. They grunted as they lifted it up to shoulder level. Addie tried to rest her corner on her shoulder, but it dug into her collarbone and hurt her. By the time they reached the front gate of the Perkins's yard, the children were huffing and puffing.

"Let's set the raft down a minute and rest," suggested Addie, breathing hard. She put her corner down, and the others followed.

"This is going to be hard," said Paul. "We still have to carry this raft past three houses before we get to Western Road."

"We can do it," Nathan encouraged. "We'll just have to walk fast, that's all. Come on! The sooner we start, the sooner we get there."

The children picked up the raft and set off again. Passing drivers craned their heads to look at the strange little group and their raft. At Western Road, the children stopped and looked carefully both ways several times before trying to cross. On the other side of the road, they put the raft down and stood looking down the steep bank

THE FIERY DRAGON GANG

at the stream below. Tall grass and thorny weeds covered the bank. The stream was a muddy brown. It didn't look like there was much water in it.

"The stream isn't as high as it was last time we came," Paul commented.

"Well, it hasn't rained for a while," Nathan said. "Naturally the water will be lower when it hasn't rained."

"How are we going to get down there?" Addie asked. The bank was so steep, it looked impossible.

"We just go down the bank," said Paul. "But watch for the thorny bushes."

"OK, I'll go down first. Addie, you can help me on the front," Nathan ordered. He turned to Con and Paul. "Hold tight to the back of the raft. Make sure it doesn't come down on top of us."

Slowly and carefully they began their descent, slipping now and then on the steep bank. Joel climbed down the bank ahead of the others and waited at the stream. He watched as the older children grunted and slipped, ouched and hollered their way down the bank. They finally arrived at the bottom, muddy, sweaty, and scratched up.

"Ow!" Addie howled. "I must have a hundred grass cuts on my legs!"

"Well, you're just lucky I didn't fall the rest of the way down the bank when I slipped," said Nathan, wiping mud off his swimming suit.

"Man, that thing is heavy!" Con exclaimed.

"Come on, you guys, let's launch this raft!" Paul reminded them. He and Con swung their side of the raft around so it was ready to slip into the stream.

"Wait! Let's move up the stream a little. It's deeper up there," suggested Nathan, standing knee-deep in the

DEADWATER RAFTING

water. The gang waded upstream to where the water reached their hips. The raft already rested in the water, but the children were still holding it up.

"OK, now let go of the raft!" said Con. The children let go, and the raft sank level with the water.

"I'm getting on," Nathan said as he hopped onto the raft. Paul joined him. The raft disappeared quickly below the surface of the stream. Joel tried to jump on, but he missed the raft and ended up standing in water up to his armpits.

"Hey, it's sinking, you guys! Get off!" Addie yelled.

"I'm not getting off," declared Paul. "What good is a raft if you can't ride on top of it?"

"It really *is* sinking." Nathan looked with dismay down at his legs, now knee-deep in brownish water. He jumped off. "Come on, Paul," he said, "get off and see if it comes back up." Paul jumped off. The gang watched in silence, hoping to see their raft pop to the surface. It didn't.

"What's the matter with it?" asked Con, groping under the water for the raft.

"Let's see if we can pull it up," Nathan said as he bent down to help Con. The children felt for the raft and tried to pull it to the surface. They pulled and grunted and strained. The raft wouldn't come up more than a foot.

Addie was the first one to let go of the raft. "It's awfully heavy," she said.

"I guess the biscuit tins are full of water by now," said Nathan mournfully.

"Maybe we used the wrong kind of wood," said Paul.

"How did Huckleberry Finn make *his* raft?" Nathan wondered. He finally let go of the raft. The other boys let go too, letting the raft sink to its watery grave.

"Maybe our pontoons weren't airtight," said Con. The

THE FIERY DRAGON GANG

children fell silent as they peered into the water, imagining they could see the raft resting in the sand at the bottom.

"Well," Addie said finally, "as long as we're here, we may as well go swimming." Joel leaped from the sandbar where he stood into deeper water. He splashed water on the others, and soon they were all playing around in the Cemetery Stream.

The next day at school, Jerry Norton asked the others, "So did you go swimming yesterday?"

"Yeah," said Nathan. "It was jolly good fun." He grinned at Jerry.

"We made a raft," Con told Jerry, "but it didn't float."

"Oh," said Jerry. "It sounds like fun." He looked wistful, and Addie suddenly felt sorry for him.

"You didn't miss much, Jerry," she told him. "The raft was as heavy as lead, and it didn't float, and we got all scratched up trying to carry it down to the stream. And then it sank. Besides, there wasn't really enough water to swim properly. You didn't miss much."

Jerry nodded and turned away, his shoulders drooping a little. "Yeah," he said.

10
The Fight

"Addie and Con, would you like some new playmates?" Dr. Barnhard asked one evening.

Addie jumped up from the couch, where she had been reading a book. "Are we getting new missionaries?" she asked eagerly. "Do they have any girls?"

"Yes, we're getting new missionaries," replied their dad with a smile. "Their names are Mr. and Mrs. Davis, and he's going to be our new hospital administrator."

"But do they have any girls?" Addie repeated her question.

"Hmmm. Let's see—any girls? No, I seem to remember they have two boys."

"Oh, no," Addie groaned. "Not more boys. I wish someone would come with girls! I'm sick of being the only girl in the school. Ever since Rachel left, I've had only boys to go to school with."

"Well, I don't mind more boys coming," said Con. "All the more to play with! Sorry, Addie!" Con added with a cheesy grin at his sister.

"I've even been praying for some girls to play with," Addie said. "Daddy, can't you tell the church to find missionaries with daughters, for a change?" But Dr. Barnhard had already walked into his air-conditioned bedroom, and Addie's complaint fell on the closed door.

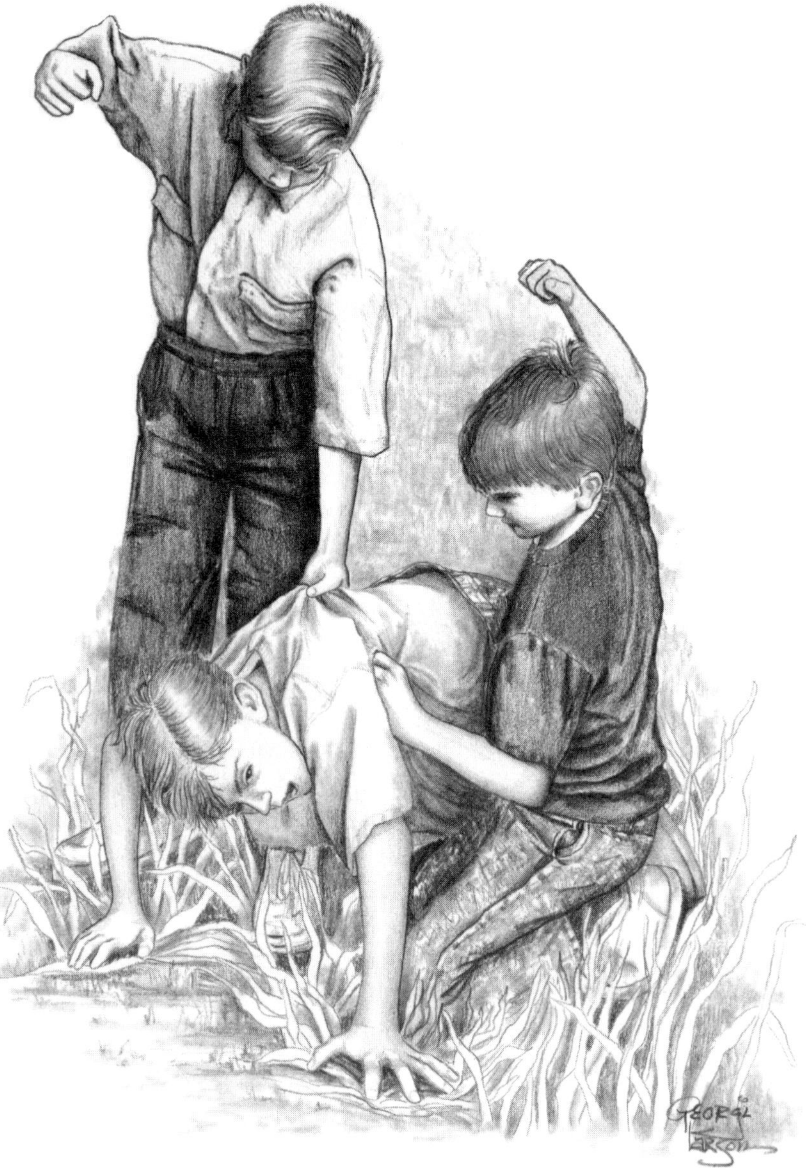

THE FIGHT

"I wonder when they're coming," Con mused. He wandered into the kitchen, where Mrs. Barnhard was busy kneading bread dough after a long day of work at the hospital. "Mama," asked Con, "do you know when the new missionaries are coming?"

"Sometime in the next week or so," Mama replied. "They've been waiting all this time for work permits from the Malaysian government. Now we've heard they've finally gotten them."

"Oh, good!" Con wandered back into the living room and picked up his book again.

The next day at school Addie and Con broke the news to the others. Miss Vanden, they discovered, had already heard about the new students. With only five students in the school now, it would make quite a difference to get two new boys.

"What grades are they going to be in?" Nathan asked Miss Vanden.

"The younger boy, Jon, will be in second grade," replied Miss Vanden. "Nicholas will be in the fourth grade with Con."

"Oh, good!" Con exclaimed, grinning. "I've never had a classmate before."

"I guess they're going to live in Rachel's old house next door. That's the one that's empty right now," said Addie, feeling a little forlorn as she remembered her friend, who had returned with her parents to the United States.

Just then Miss Vanden called the children back to their studies. "We need to get back on track with Bible class now." She walked over to the felt board, and soon the children were caught up in the Bible story about Samson.

At recess time that morning, the children decided to play dare base. Nathan and Paul were chosen as team captains, and they began picking team members.

THE FIERY DRAGON GANG

"I'll take Jerry," said Nathan.

"No fair," complained Paul. "You got first picks, and you and Jerry are the fastest runners."

"OK, then you take Addie and Con," said Nathan.

"What about my sister?" said Jerry, pointing toward his house. "She's just coming out to play with us."

"You can take Kamie, Nathan," said Paul, looking as though he was pleased with his generous offer. "Then we'll be even up, three and three."

"Kamie won't help much. All she ever does is stick to the base like glue," Nathan replied with disgust. "Oh, well, never mind. Our base is the flame tree over here. You take that second mangosteen tree over there." Nathan gestured toward the mangosteen tree nearest to the swing set. Miss Vanden, seeing that the children had their game set up, walked over to the edge of the field, where she could stand and supervise.

The children took their places, and soon they were daring and chasing one another between the two bases. Out of the corner of her eye, Addie saw Jerry sneaking along the fence toward their base. She dashed back to the mangosteen tree and tagged up before chasing Jerry back toward his own base at the flame tree. Just as she tagged up again, Addie saw Con getting close to the other base. "Con, be careful!" she yelled. At that moment Nathan tagged up and sprinted after Con. Addie took off toward the two boys. Nathan, warned off by Addie's approach, did a U-turn, heading back to the flame tree to tag up again.

For a while, the children played carefully, staying close to their own bases. Then Jerry decided to show some bravery. He crept closer to the mangosteen tree than before.

"Nah, nah! Can't catch me," Jerry sang out. Then he

THE FIGHT

put his thumbs in his ears and waggled his fingers at Paul's team. At the same time he stuck his tongue out rudely at them.

"Jerry, you twit! Get back here," Nathan yelled at him from the base.

Jerry ignored him. "Nah, nah—nah nah nah," he sang out again, jumping one step closer to his opponents' base.

"*Jerry!*" Nathan yelled warningly.

"Jerry, come on!" Kamie pleaded from beside Nathan.

Con jumped off base and took a swipe at Jerry. Jerry hopped back, arching his back so that Con's swing just missed where his stomach had been. He ran a few steps backward, laughing. "Nah, nah, can't catch me," he taunted.

Suddenly Paul sprinted off base with unusual speed and tagged Jerry hard on the shoulder.

"*Hey!*" Jerry yelled, his face turning crimson. "You're not supposed to hit me." He ran after Paul and thumped him hard on the back with both fists.

"*Ouch!*" Paul yelled, slumping to the ground. "Ow, ow, ow! Miss Vanden!"

Miss Vanden ran over to check on Paul. When she saw that Paul could sit up, she called Jerry to her and began giving him a talking to. Paul sat on the ground, his face screwed up with pain. The other children could see that he was trying to blink back the tears as they gathered around him.

"Paul, are you going to be all right?" asked Nathan anxiously. He patted his brother's shoulder with sympathy.

Addie looked up to see Jerry walking down the road toward the schoolhouse. "Miss Vanden must have sent him back to the school to sit down," she thought.

99

THE FIERY DRAGON GANG

"Jerry, you *idiot,*" Nathan yelled furiously at Jerry's retreating figure. "We're going to get you back, just wait and see." His face was bright red with anger.

"Now, Nathan," Miss Vanden said sternly. "That's not the way to act. You may not call people names."

"Well, he hurt my brother!" Nathan protested, still angry.

"Maybe so, but getting revenge won't help," replied Miss Vanden. "Just let him be." She pulled Paul to his feet and helped him over to the side of the field. Nathan, Addie, and Con followed, while Kamie drifted silently off toward home. It was no use having any more recesses with only three players left.

Nathan gave Jerry dirty looks throughout the rest of the day in school. Paul seemed to be fully recovered, but Nathan wasn't going to forget that his brother had suffered because of the Fiery Dragon Gang's enemy.

Jerry knew he was in trouble with Nathan. He left for home as soon as he was excused at the end of the school day. As soon as Jerry was out the door, Nathan called the other children together. "We've got to teach Jerry a lesson," he announced. "He had no right to beat up on you, Paul."

"Well, I think that Jerry thought Paul hit him first, when he tagged him," Con said. "He was mad because of that."

"I didn't hit him," Paul protested. "I just touched him, like this." He tapped Con lightly on the shoulder. "Does that hurt?"

"No," Con admitted.

"Well, then, why did he have to go and get so raving loony about it?" asked Paul.

"I think we should go and teach him a lesson," Nathan said. "Are you guys coming?"

THE FIGHT

"Sure," said Paul.

"Well, he deserves being taught a lesson, anyway," said Addie slowly. She wondered what kind of lesson the boys planned to teach Jerry.

Nathan started off, with Paul behind him. Addie hesitated, and then followed, curious as to what they were going to do. Con lingered behind.

"Hey, Con," Nathan called back. "Are you coming or not?" Con, not answering, stood still for a few seconds. Then he slowly walked toward them.

The children walked over to the Norton's house, next door to the school. Nathan rapped on the back door, which the Nortons used as their main entry. No one answered the door. Nathan knocked again.

"I don't think anyone can hear you," Addie said. "Try the doorbell." She reached up and pushed the doorbell as she peered through the screen in the top half of the door. There was no sound from inside the house.

"Let's try the front door," suggested Nathan, turning and heading around the corner. "I'm sure he's home; he just left school a few minutes ago." The children paraded around to the Nortons' front double doors. Nathan knocked on the door. Peering through the sheer curtains hung behind the screens, the children spied a movement back in the hallway.

"Jerry, we know you're there," called Nathan. "Come on out here."

Jerry emerged from the hall and came to the front doors. "What do you want?" he asked suspiciously.

"We want to talk to you," said Nathan, his voice sounding friendly. "Come on out."

Jerry unbolted the front door and swung it open. "Yeah?" he asked warily.

Addie noticed the glance that passed between Nathan

THE FIERY DRAGON GANG

and Paul. Suddenly the two boys jumped on Jerry. Nathan and Paul each grabbed one of Jerry's arms and dragged him down onto the porch.

"Hey! What are you doing?" Jerry yelled, struggling to get free. "Let me go!"

"No, we won't," Nathan replied through gritted teeth. He and Paul began dragging Jerry toward the gardenia bush on the far side of the house. "We're going to teach you a lesson you won't forget. You don't go about beating on members of our Fiery Dragon Gang."

Addie and Con both stood back. Their mouths hung open as they watched the turn of events. They had never guessed that this was Nathan and Paul's idea of "teaching a lesson." Without realizing it, they followed the struggling boys to the side of the house that was away from the compound road. Nathan was thumping on Jerry's back with his free arm. On the other side, Paul grimly dragged Jerry along, holding onto one arm with both hands.

"Let me go, you idiots!" Jerry yelled at the top of his lungs. He twisted back and forth, trying to free himself. "Ouch! Stop it!" He kicked out, his foot catching Nathan in the shin.

"*Ow!*" Nathan yelled. "Now we're *really* going to teach you!" Nathan tripped Jerry up with one foot, and Jerry landed in the grass with a thud. Nathan and Paul, nearly losing their grip, went down on the grass with Jerry. Both had turned red in the face, and Nathan's hair was falling over his eyes. "Come help us hold him, Con," he called, pausing to look in Con and Addie's direction.

Con and Addie stood as if rooted to the ground. Suddenly a man's voice boomed out behind them. *"Just what do you think you're doing?"*

THE FIGHT

The children whirled around to see Dr. Norton on the porch dressed in his slacks and undershirt, his feet bare. Nathan and Paul froze. Jerry froze. Suddenly Addie felt as if she had unfrozen. She felt a pang shoot through her chest; it always happened when she became frightened. She clutched at the sides of her skirt and stared at Dr. Norton.

"What's going on here?" Dr. Norton demanded, advancing forward. He looked very mean and very unhappy.

Nathan jumped up. "Uh—I know things don't look too good here, Dr. Norton," he began.

"Look good!" Dr. Norton bellowed. "Things look pretty bad, if you ask me. Here I'm peacefully taking a nap on my afternoon off, and I'm rudely awakened by you children beating up on my son. Jerry, just what has been going on?"

"Well, Dr. Norton," Nathan began again, trying to speak before Jerry got a word in.

"Nathan, be quiet," Dr. Norton said angrily. He walked over to Jerry and took him by the arm, still looking at Nathan and Paul. "Don't even try making excuses. Children, I'm very, very angry with all of you. This is a despicable way to behave. Nathan and Paul, you can be very sure I'm going to ring up your father on the telephone. I shall tell him just what I've seen here. Addie and Con, I don't know what part you had in this, but I'm very disappointed to see you two mixed up in this behavior as well."

Addie looked away, feeling like a meaner, nastier person with every word Dr. Norton uttered. Con stood quietly beside her, looking glumly at his feet. Addie didn't dare look over at Nathan and Paul. Stealing a look at Jerry, she saw the rumpled boy watching his father. He

103

THE FIERY DRAGON GANG

blinked his eyes nervously.

Dr. Norton walked Jerry back toward the front doors of their house. Then he turned. "You children can leave now. Don't let me catch you lurking around our house again." With that, he marched Jerry into the house.

Silently the Fiery Dragon Gang turned toward the school.

"He wouldn't even listen to me," Nathan finally burst out. The other children didn't answer. Addie, feeling miserable, looked over at Con. He looked just as upset as she felt. He returned her look and sighed heavily. Addie knew he was trying to hold back tears.

Reaching the school, Nathan and Paul unlocked their bicycles and walked them out to the compound road. "Well, we're in for it when we get home," Paul said at last.

"I'm going to tell Dad the whole story," Nathan announced. "Jerry deserved every bit of what he got, and more. He's just a mean, hot-tempered person. I hope we taught him a lesson."

"But I don't think we should have done that," said Con slowly.

"Well, *you're* safe," said Paul. "You didn't do anything."

"We were there, and Dr. Norton saw us," Addie said, understanding her brother's feeling of sharing the responsibility in what had happened.

"Aw, you don't need to worry," said Nathan. "Paul, we'd better get home. I want to talk to Dad before Dr. Norton gets to him. Else he's going to be ripping mad at us."

Nathan and Paul mounted their bicycles and headed for the gate. Con and Addie walked slowly home. Silently they climbed the back stairs and entered their

THE FIGHT

house. Con walked into the living room and plopped down onto the firm blue cushions of the couch. "We really shouldn't have been there, Addie," he said. "You know that."

"I know," Addie replied. "I guess I didn't think Nathan and Paul would actually beat up on him."

Both children sat still for a minute, thinking over what had happened. Then, with a sigh, Con rose from the couch and went to his room. Addie couldn't seem to get away from the scenes running through her mind. She walked over to the piano bench and sat down to practice. But running through her piano scales didn't seem to ease her mind. It seemed as though the phrase ran through her head in a rhythm, "You shouldn't have gone along. You shouldn't have been there. You shouldn't have gone along. . . ."

11
Turned Tables

Addie and Con waited on the front steps of the school the next morning, watching for Nathan and Paul to arrive. Miss Vanden rang the first bell for the warning that school would start in five minutes.

"Where are they?" Addie fretted, looking up the road toward the gate.

"They're just late, as usual," Con said, turning to go into the classroom. "Come on, Addie. You'll be counted late if you're not in your seat."

Addie entered the classroom and sat down, lifting her desktop to take out her pencil. Then she remembered that it was her turn to hand out the green songbooks for worship that week. She was just putting the last songbook in place when she heard Nathan and Paul ride up outside. Glancing at Jerry, who was sitting quietly at his desk, Addie slipped out the door.

"What happened?" Addie hissed at Nathan.

Nathan rolled his eyes at her and then turned to lock his bicycle. "It was horrid," he said in a low tone. "Dad was ripping ticked off at us." He looked up as Con stepped out of the door to ring the last bell. "I'll tell you later," Nathan said as he and Addie rushed into the classroom.

After lunch the Fiery Dragon Gang got together to

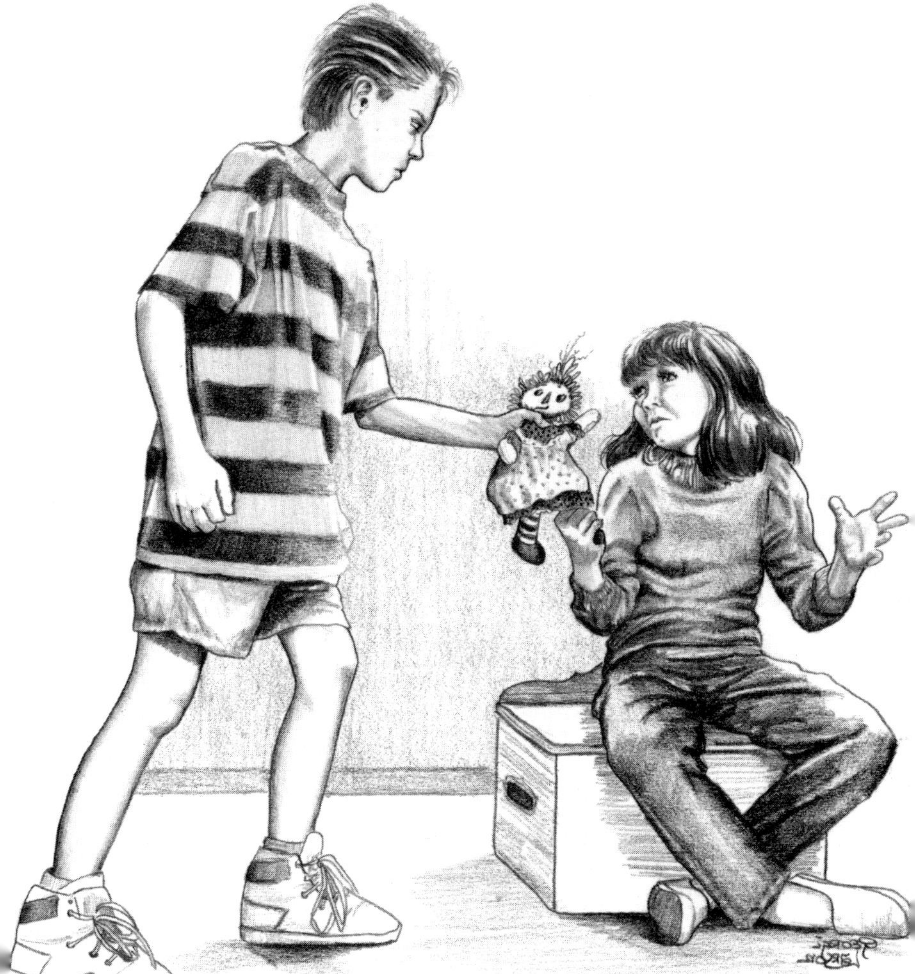

THE FIERY DRAGON GANG

talk things over. They all met at the Barnhard house, and together they started walking toward school for the afternoon session.

"So, what did your dad say?" Con asked, unable to wait any longer.

"Well, he was terribly unhappy with us," Nathan began.

"He said we can't have the Fiery Dragon Gang anymore," Paul interrupted.

"Paul! I'm telling them!" Nathan protested.

"Sorry," said Paul, not sounding very sorry.

"Anyhow, as Paul said, it all comes down to this: we can't belong to the gang anymore, and we're not allowed to go to the pool for a week as punishment."

"Well, if you can't be in the gang, then there's no use having a gang with just Con and me," said Addie.

"I don't want to be in a gang anyhow," said Con, as though he'd already made the decision.

"I think it's just too bad," said Nathan. "Our Fiery Dragon Gang was a good idea."

"Well, Dad said that a club is fine, but we shouldn't have chosen an enemy," said Paul.

"Yeah," said Addie slowly. She wasn't sure which of Dr. Perkins's statements she was agreeing with. She was just relieved it hadn't become a bigger incident than it already was.

The children reached the climbing tree. Con shinned up the tree, with the others close behind.

"I still think a club is a great idea," said Nathan, pulling himself up from branch to branch.

"Too bad your dad outlawed it," said Addie.

Nathan looked thoughtful. "He didn't outlaw it, really," he began. "He just said we couldn't keep people out of a club."

TURNED TABLES

"Nathan," Paul protested. "Dad said we had to quit having the Fiery Dragon Gang!"

"I know," Nathan said. "I guess one can't get around that."

The punishment wasn't too hard to take, since many of the Fiery Dragon Gang schemes had not worked out. The worst part was that Nathan and Paul couldn't go to the pool for a week. That was punishment for Addie and Con as well, since they always got their rides to the pool with the Perkinses.

However, the punishment was soon forgotten in the excitement of Friday. On Friday the Davises, the new missionaries from America, arrived. Since their plane came in during school time Friday morning, the children couldn't go out to the airport to meet the new family. But Addie came to school with the news that they would see the Davises at church, and the missionaries would all be getting together for a potluck after church to welcome them.

The children got to church early and hurried in. They immediately picked out the two new boys. The brothers were sitting quietly next to each other, waiting for the program to start. The older boy was skinny and had his blond hair neatly slicked back. His younger brother had a pug nose and a round face topped by light brown hair shaved in a crew cut. His hair was greased so that the spikes stood straight up.

Addie and Con, suddenly feeling a little shy, sat down in the row behind the boys. For a minute or two things were quiet, while Addie wondered what she should say. Then the leaders began the program, and from then on things were too busy to talk.

When they got home from church, Addie and Con's mom called them to the kitchen. "Kids," said Dr.

THE FIERY DRAGON GANG

Barnhard, "I need your help to put extra leaves in the table and set things out. Addie, will you take care of setting the table? Con, you can peel the carrots for me and make the drink."

The children got busy with their lunch duties, and soon the other missionary families began to arrive for the potluck. Addie had set up a table downstairs on the back patio, where the children could eat. After the blessing the children went through line for their food first. Carefully balancing their plates and cups of juice, they made their way downstairs and out into the sunshine. The Davis boys, looking shy, were the last ones to arrive with their food. Mrs. Perkins bustled down the stairs with them, getting them placed at the table and making sure they didn't need anything else.

"Hullo," said Nathan, tilting his head slightly as he eyed the new boys. "I'm Nathan."

"I'm Nicolas, and this is Jon," said the older boy with a drawl.

"Where did you come from?" Nathan asked as Paul came up to the table and joined him.

"We're from Menard, Texas," Jon said proudly.

"I've heard of Texas, but I've never heard of Menard," said Addie, leaning forward. She felt rather proud, being a fellow American to Nicolas and Jon.

"This is Addie," said Nathan, introducing her. "And that's Con."

"Hi," said Nicolas.

"I'm Paul. His brother," Paul said, pointing at Nathan. "We're from Australia," he added proudly.

"I'm from Australia too," Jerry broke in. "I'm Jerry, and this is Kamie. She's my sister."

"I can hear your accent," Nicolas said politely.

"We're Americans, but Con and I have never lived

TURNED TABLES

there," said Addie. "We were born after our parents came over here as missionaries."

"Oh," said Nicolas. "Well, it's nice to have other Americans here." Jon nodded.

Addie saw Nathan straighten up defensively on his chair as he was left out of the American group. He looked as though he were about to give a quick retort. He stopped himself, paused, and began, "Well, it's jolly good you chaps have come. We need more kids in our school. It will be a lot more fun at recess with you guys here."

"How many kids go to your school?" asked Nicolas.

"Just us five," Paul said, waving his arm at the others. "Kamie isn't in school yet."

Nicolas looked startled. "Just you? Just five kids? That's a pretty small school. In Texas we went to a big school."

"Well, it's not as bad as it sounds," said Addie, feeling defensive. It seemed that these new boys were going to compare everything to Texas. Perhaps they would think Penang wasn't as good.

"We have lots of fun here," Paul said cheerfully, "and there are lots of fun things to do around Penang."

"Like what?" asked Jon.

"Well, we belong to a swimming club, for starters," said Nathan. "It has a fifty-meter pool. We'll take you with us sometime soon. Paul and I compete in the swim meets there. Addie and Con don't compete," he added disdainfully.

Addie felt a little hurt at Nathan's tone of voice. "Well, we go just for fun—" she began.

"And if you like swimming at beaches, there are lots of those," interrupted Nathan.

"Is the ocean far away?" asked Nicolas, looking interested.

111

THE FIERY DRAGON GANG

"No," Addie answered him. "We're about a mile from the ocean—"

"But the water is really dirty and mucky there," Nathan interrupted again. "We have to drive about half an hour to get to the nice beaches past the swimming club. We'll take you there too."

"What else do you do?" Jon asked. "Do you play softball or anything?"

"We could at recess," said Nathan. "But we're from Australia, so when we're home we play cricket or soccer."

"There's also Youth Park," Con began.

"Oh, yeah," said Nathan, not looking at Con. "We go skating at Youth Park, and there's an obstacle course there."

"It's fun to go on it," said Paul. "It's built like military training courses for jungle warfare." He grinned triumphantly at the expectant looks on the Davis boys' faces.

"I can't wait to go on an obstacle course!" Jon said.

"Me too!" Nicolas joined in.

As the children finished their lunch, Addie didn't say much more. Nathan was ignoring her and Con, and giving all his attention to the new boys. Jerry and Kamie were also being left out, but that was usual. Nathan and Paul were inviting Nicolas and Jon to come over and play at their house—and weren't saying anything about inviting the others to come as well. Addie began to feel more and more left out. She felt awful.

It began to get terribly hot in the sunshine, so the boys headed for Con's room when they had finished dessert. Con's room had an air conditioner and a ceiling fan, giving some relief from the midday heat. Addie stopped by the kitchen to drop off the last of the plates from the kitchen table. Then she and Kamie went to Con's room to join the boys.

TURNED TABLES

Nathan gave the girls a hostile look as they entered the room. "Why don't you go play somewhere else?" he suggested rudely.

"We want to come see what you're doing," replied Addie.

"Well, maybe we want to play with just Nicolas and Jon, without you," Nathan said.

"Oh, come on, Nathan," Addie pleaded. Kamie moved a step closer to Addie.

Nathan, getting tired of harassing the girls, flopped on the bed. Addie's Raggedy Ann lay by the pillow. Addie had set the doll there before she left for church. Mrs. Barnhard's old friend in America, Mrs. Weller, had hand-stitched the rag doll for Addie. Addie had often heard her mother say that this handmade Raggedy Ann was special. Mrs. Weller was practically blind in both eyes and had spent hours embroidering the eyes, nose, and mouth on Raggedy Ann's face.

Nathan picked up the rag doll and turned it over in his hands. Addie suddenly realized that an idea was forming in Nathan's mind, but she was too late to stop it. Nathan idly threw Raggedy Ann into the air and caught her.

"Nathan!" Addie cried. "Give me my Raggedy Ann." She noticed that Nicolas and Jon were snickering. That egged Nathan on. He threw Raggedy Ann up in the air again, this time a little higher.

"Nathan, please!" Addie pleaded. "Leave her alone."

"Ha, ha! Maybe she wants to fly," said Nathan, throwing the doll into the air yet again.

"*Nathan!*" Addie yelled, tears of anger popping into her eyes. She grabbed for the rag doll, but missed.

"Ha, ha, ha! Come and rescue your precious dolly," Nathan teased, while Jon, Nicolas, Paul, and Con

113

THE FIERY DRAGON GANG

laughed. Up went Raggedy Ann again. This time, to Addie's horror, the doll landed on a blade of the ceiling fan. She hung high up there, out of reach.

"Nathan, you meany!" Addie yelled, angry and crying at the same time. "That's my special Raggedy Ann. My mom's blind friend made her."

"OK, OK!" Nathan exclaimed. "Calm down. She's all yours now."

"I can't get her down," Addie sobbed. "She's too high up." Addie dropped onto the bed and cried as Kamie awkwardly patted her on the shoulder.

"Look at her, crying over a stupid rag doll," Nathan taunted. The other boys were quiet now, seeing that Addie was really distressed.

"Knock it off, Nathan," Con said, pulling his desk chair under the fan. "Calm down, Addie. We'll get it down." He stepped up on the chair and reached as high as he could, but he couldn't reach the doll perched on the blade of the ceiling fan.

"Here, let me try," said Nathan. "I'm taller than you." He stepped up on the chair and stretched up toward the doll, but he couldn't reach her either.

Addie sat watching him, tears still streaming down her cheeks. "How are we going to get her down?" she asked.

"It's easy. Just turn on the fan," said Paul suddenly from his seat on the other bed. "Then she'll fly off."

"No!" Addie exclaimed. "She'll get hurt!"

"Oh, Addie, be reasonable. She's just a doll," Nathan said impatiently as he flipped the fan switch.

The children watched, transfixed, as the fan began to turn, slowly at first, and then faster and faster. Raggedy Ann's hair began to blow in the breeze as she whirled around and around on the fan blade. Watching her made

114

TURNED TABLES

Addie dizzy. She began to feel sick. Her Raggedy Ann was like a friend, and she watched in horror as the doll became a blur on the spinning fan.

Suddenly Raggedy Ann flew off the fan and landed with an undignified *plunk* in the far corner of the room. The boys cheered and hooted as Addie ran over to pick up her doll tenderly.

Seeing a streak of dirt across Raggedy Ann's hand-embroidered face, Addie felt anger churn again in her stomach. "Nathan," she began. Then she stopped, not knowing quite how to put her anger into words. Much to her dismay, she began to cry again. She gulped down a sob and continued. "You are so *mean*. You leave people out of things, and you hurt their feelings. And—and—I think you're the meanest boy in the whole world," she blubbered. She turned and ran out of the room, slamming the door behind her.

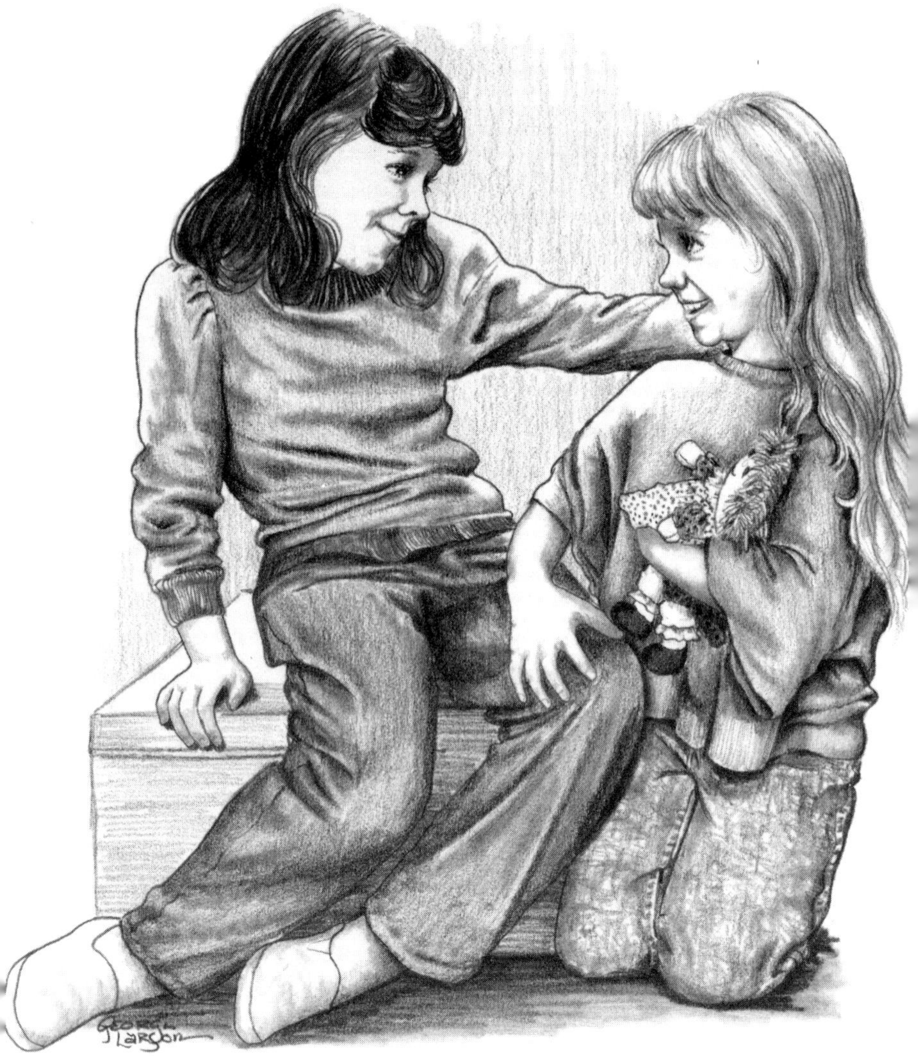
George
Larson

12
Do Unto Others

As Addie ran out of Con's room and into the hallway, tears streaming down her face, she hadn't decided where to go. She paused a moment, knowing that all the adults were in the living room and kitchen. Not wanting the adults to see her upset, she ran down the hallway to her own room, closing her door behind her. Flopping down on the bed, Addie let the tears take over.

"Nathan makes me so mad," she thought angrily. "He has been mean to me ever since they came over for lunch. He's just leaving me out, and he's not going to let me play with the others. At least Con is a boy, so he can join in on the fun."

Addie propped herself up on her elbows to look at her Raggedy Ann, which she had been clutching to herself. She tried rubbing off the dirt streak on Raggedy Ann's face, but her wet fingers only smeared it more. Addie thought of old almost-blind Mrs. Weller, carefully embroidering the eyes, nose, and mouth on the rag doll for a little missionary girl halfway around the world. Mama had said that Mrs. Weller probably wouldn't make any more rag dolls, ever, since her sight was gone by now, and she was very old. The thought made Addie start crying harder again.

THE FIERY DRAGON GANG

The door opened, and Mrs. Barnhard popped her head into Addie's room. "Addie!" she exclaimed. "What's the matter?" She came over and sat down on the bed beside her daughter.

"Oh, Mama, I'm so m-mad at Nathan," Addie sobbed, hiccuping on some of her words. "He's not letting m-me join the others, and he th-threw my Raggedy Ann doll up on the f-fan!" Addie scooted over on the bed to put her head in her mother's lap.

"What do you mean, he's not letting you join the others?" Mrs. Barnhard asked.

"W-well," Addie sniffled, "he told Kamie and me to go and p-play somewhere else, and then he snatched my R-raggedy Ann and started throwing her around, and then she g-got stuck on the fan."

"Oh, Addie," Mrs. Barnhard said sympathetically, patting her daughter on the shoulder and brushing her hair back soothingly.

"And, Mama, you said Mrs. Weller worked so hard on my doll when she was almost blind," Addie continued, "and look here. See this streak?" Addie pointed to the dirty smear across Raggedy Ann's face. "That's from the dirt on top of the fan."

Mrs. Barnhard examined the streak. "I don't think Nathan was very nice to do that to your doll," she said, rubbing her finger across the dirt, "but I think we can get the dirt off, Addie."

"You can?" Addie asked hopefully.

"I think so," her mother said. "Take it down to the laundry room this afternoon, and I'll work on it tonight or tomorrow."

"Oh, Mama, thank you," Addie said gratefully, wiping her nose on the back of her hand.

"Everything all right now?" Mrs. Barnhard asked.

DO UNTO OTHERS

"Well, sort of," Addie said. "But I still don't like what Nathan did to me, telling Kamie and me to go away and not play with them and the Davis boys. I feel left out."

"That doesn't feel very good, I know," Mrs. Barnhard agreed. "Sometimes people do that to us, though, because people can be cruel. What do you think you can do about it?"

"I don't know," Addie said.

Suddenly a thought struck Addie like a thunderbolt. She was feeling the same way that Jerry Norton had felt all this time when the other children were leaving him out of the Fiery Dragon Gang! He had felt left out and unwanted. He had felt like this when Nathan told him to go away. He had felt like others were treating him unfairly and bothering him just to have fun at his expense. "How awful," Addie thought. "I'm feeling just like Jerry has been feeling, and here I was one of the Fiery Dragon Gang doing all those things to him and leaving him out of things. I should have followed the golden rule: 'Do unto others as you would have them do unto you.'"

Addie's mother, not knowing why her daughter was so quiet, said, "Well, it might help you to think of what Jesus would do if people left Him out of things."

"Yeah. I don't know," said Addie in a subdued tone of voice. She wasn't ready to tell her mother what she had just been thinking about. She realized that Mrs. Barnhard hadn't even known about the Fiery Dragon Gang. The children had all agreed from the start to keep it a secret. "Mum's the word," they had said.

Just then there came a soft knock at the door. Kamie slipped into the room and came over to Addie. Glancing shyly sideways at Addie's mother, she asked Addie, "Are you all right now?"

"Yes." Addie took a deep breath and heaved a long,

THE FIERY DRAGON GANG

shaky sigh. "I guess so."

"Well, Addie," her mother said, rising from her seat on the bed. "I need to get back to our guests. But I think you need to figure out a good way to handle the situation when people leave you out of things, and don't let it bother you so much." She gave her daughter a meaningful look. "OK?" she asked.

Addie managed a crooked half-smile. "OK, Mama," she replied.

When Mrs. Barnhard had left the room, closing the door behind her, Addie turned to Kamie.

"What are you going to do now?" Kamie asked.

"Well, since the boys won't let us play with them, let's figure out something we can do to have fun together," Addie suggested, rubbing her face to get rid of the tear marks. Then she continued a little more shyly, "Kamie, I know what it feels like now when people tell you to go away and not play with them. I'm sorry for the times we haven't let you and Jerry play with us."

"You're forgiven," said Kamie sweetly. "It's OK."

"I'm never, ever, ever going to be in a club again," said Addie firmly. "At least I'm not going to be in a club that leaves anybody out. It's just not nice, and it's not Christian." She glanced at Kamie, who seemed a little puzzled by all that she was saying. "She's too little to really understand what I'm talking about," Addie thought. She sighed another long sigh, and then an idea came to her mind, and her face brightened. "Kamie, I have an idea," she said, taking Kamie's hand. "I read this story in *Uncle Arthur's Bedtime Stories* about the Surprise Package Company. We can do something, just the two of us, and it won't be a club."

"What's a Surprise Package Company?" asked Kamie.

"It's when a person or a few people get together and

DO UNTO OTHERS

make surprise packages for people. Then you wrap them up or put them in a basket, and you put them on someone's doorstep and ring the doorbell and run away."

"Oh, that sounds like fun!" Kamie exclaimed.

"It must be lots of fun. You can't imagine how many people were cheered up because of the Surprise Package Company in *Uncle Arthur's Bedtime Stories*," said Addie enthusiastically.

"What could we put in the packages?" asked Kamie.

"We could pick flowers," said Addie. "There are lots of them in our backyard, and orchids too. They last a long time."

"Who are we going to give them to?" Kamie asked.

"Who do you think we should give them to?" Addie wondered. "Maybe Miss Vanden, for one. She lives all alone."

"Yeah," Kamie agreed. "And could we put one on Miss Newton's door?"

Addie remembered the head nurse, who also lived alone on the hospital compound. "Sure," she said. "Let's start with them, and then we can think of some more."

"Can we do it now?" Kamie asked.

"Why not? Let's sneak out the back door and go on a flower hunt," Addie suggested.

Hand in hand, the girls opened the bedroom door, peered into the hallway, and then quietly sneaked out through the living room and dining room on their secret mission. "It feels good to be doing something kind to someone else for a change," thought Addie. "I think the Fiery Dragon Gang has taught me an important lesson about treating others the way I would want to be treated." Addie tightened her grip on Kamie's hand. "Come on," she whispered. "Let's hurry up. We have a lot to do!"

121

You'll love 'em!

Treasures by the Sea, by Sally Streib

Eric and his twin sister Susan didn't want to leave home and live with their Aunt Myrtle at her California beach house. But Mom had died, and Dad thought it best for the twins to stay with their aunt for a while.

Eric and Susan never felt so lonely.

But discovery and delight gradually replace the hurt and loneliness as Aunt Myrtle wisely uses lessons from nature to teach the twins about a God who loves and cares for them.

US$6.95/Cdn$8.70. Paper, 160 pages.

Thunder, the Maverick Mustang, by Nora Ann Kuehn

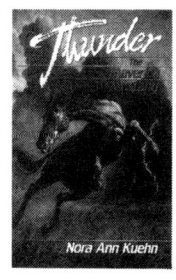

Ken and his brother Bob worked hard on old man Weese's ranch to earn the black mustang. Ken loved the fiery pony with all his heart, but Thunder refused to be tamed. Ken was stubborn too. He would win the pony's affections with kindness no matter what.

Just when Thunder begins to calm down, a forest fire burns the fence posts, and he escapes. Is Ken's love strong enough to make the black mustang come home?

US$6.95/Cdn$8.70. Paper, 96 pages.

Please photocopy and complete the form below.

❏ **Treasures by the Sea**
   US$6.95/Cdn$8.70.

❏ **Thunder, the Maverick Mustang**
   US$6.95/Cdn$8.70.

Please add applicable sales tax and 15% (US$2.50 minimum) to cover postage and handling.

Name _____

Address _____

City _____

State _____ Zip _____

Price	$ _____	Order from your Adventist Book Center, or ABC
Postage	$ _____	Mailing Service, P.O. Box 7000, Boise, Idaho
Sales Tax	$ _____	83707. Prices subject to change without notice.
TOTAL	$ _____	Make check payable to Adventist Book Center.

© 1990 Pacific Press Publishing Association 2295

Who is Becka Bailey?

If you don't know her, hurry and get acquainted with the little girl with a bright future from the Pacific Northwest.

The ***Becka Bailey Series***, by Paula Montgomery, follows Becka's journey from child to adulthood in four enchanting books.

Coyotes in the Wind captures Becka's early years in her mountain home. Blizzards, fires, caring for a retarded child, and an erupting volcano help teach Becka that God is working in her life.

New friends, dorm life, and first love make Becka's freshman year in academy one to remember in ***Down the River Road***.

Becka finally realizes her dream to be a summer-camp counselor. ***A Summer to Grow On*** is filled with the excitement of camp life and tells of a secret romance with a fellow counselor.

When November Comes finds Becka in college sharing her love for camp counseling with someone very special. Could God have brought them together for a reason?

Meet Becka Bailey and see God at work in the life of an energetic young person.

US$24.95/Cdn$31.20 for four-book set.
Please photocopy and complete the form below.

❑ The *Becka Bailey Series*
US$24.95/Cdn$31.20.

Please add applicable sales tax and 15% (US$2.50 minimum) to cover postage and handling.

Name _____

Address _____

City _____

State _____ Zip _____

Price $ _____   Order from your Adventist Book Center, or ABC
Postage $ _____   Mailing Service, P.O. Box 7000, Boise, Idaho
Sales Tax $ _____   83707. Prices subject to change without notice.
TOTAL $ _____   Make check payable to Adventist Book Center.

© 1990 Pacific Press Publishing Association 2229